Marketing for Complementary Therapists

Practical books that inspire

Learning to Counsel
How to develop the skills to work effectively with others

Working with Dreams
Understand your dreams and use them for personal and creative development

Asserting Your Self
How to feel more confident about getting more from life

Making the Most of Your Relationships
How to find satisfaction and intimacy with family and friends

Please send for a free copy of the latest catalogue to:

How To Books
3 Newtec Place, Magdalen Road
Oxford OX4 1RE, United Kingdom
email: info@howtobooks.co.uk
http://www.howtobooks.co.uk

Marketing for Complementary Therapists

101 tried and tested ways to attract clients

STEVEN A. HAROLD

howtobooks

Published in 2002 by How To Books Ltd,
3 Newtec Place, Magdalen Road,
Oxford OX4 1RE, United Kingdom.
Tel: (01865) 793806. Fax: (01865) 248780.
email: info@howtobooks.co.uk
http://www.howtobooks.co.uk

First edition published 2002
Reprinted 2003

British Library Cataloguing in Publication Data.
A catalogue record for this book is available from
the British Library.

Cover design by Baseline Arts Ltd, Oxford

Produced for How To Books by Deer Park Productions
Edited by Francesca Mitchell
Typeset by Kestrel Data, Exeter, Devon
Printed and bound by Cromwell Press Ltd, Trowbridge, Wiltshire

NOTE: The material contained in this book is set out in good
faith for general guidance and no liability can be accepted
for loss or expense incurred as a result of relying in particular
circumstances on statements made in the book. Laws and
regulations are complex and liable to change, and readers should
check the current position with the relevant authorities before
making personal arrangements.

Contents

In Memory of

Dr. David Allen Page
1942–2000

*'We are what we are
and we do what we do.'*

Acknowledgements

I would like to thank the many people who have played a part in bringing this book into existence. To Terence Watts for being my unofficial mentor in my early days of practice. Nicola Martin of the Institute of Clinical Hypnosis for providing the opportunity to change my dreams into reality. Pauline and Dennis Yates for being my editors. My parents Raymond and Mavourneen for always being there. Lastly, my special thanks must go to John for his encouragement, support and belief in me.

Preface

Today there are hundreds of alternative and complementary therapies available to the general public as well as the more conventional therapies of psychotherapy or counselling. The vast majority of these therapies are not available through your doctor. They have to be sought out. To benefit from these therapies the public has to find therapists who are in private practice.

As well as the existence of many different types of therapy, there are also hundreds of schools offering training on how to become a therapist in any chosen subject – from acupuncture to reiki, from kinesiology to naturopathy – there are many options with which to make your trade in the alternative and conventional medicine arena. You can take a correspondence course, a course over a period of years or an intensive course over a period of days and at the end call yourself a therapist. A course should not be judged by the period of time involved. Some of the best and most skilful therapists are self-taught and have never seen the inside of a classroom since leaving school.

Whichever way you become competent in your skill, you will have one major lesson to learn when you graduate: how to attract clients to your practice. Some schools do an excellent job of providing their graduates with the necessary business skills to enable them to taste success quickly. Others do not provide an adequate grounding or the type of continued support necessary to help a fledgling therapist move from seeing an occasional client to having a full-time practice. Many therapy graduates have expectations of becoming a full-time therapist. They may see an opportunity of moving from a career that bores them to something more exciting. Without appropriate marketing skills, they are likely to fail and will probably return to their old career or at best have a very part-time business in which they occasionally attract a client or two.

You should not jump from a full-time career to self-employment in one leap unless you have a safety net in place! The safety net could be a redundancy lump sum, a supportive partner or other funding to help you while you get your practice up and running. If you don't have any of these then you should consider reducing your hours in the old profession as you increase the hours in the new career. You could negotiate a reduction in the hours with your current employer such as moving from a five-day week to four days. As your therapy practice expands over a period of time, you can reduce the hours you spend in the old career, eventually making a complete career change. This approach brings the comfort of knowing you have another source of income and takes away some of the financial pressure from your therapy practice.

Being a successful therapist, particularly in private practice, requires good marketing skills. It is no good being the most effective therapist in the world if you don't tell the world that you exist. Your practice will be a success or failure depending on your therapy and marketing skills. Most therapists have to find out the hard way what works for them and what doesn't.

Some new therapists fall into the trap of attempting to 'buy' their clients, in effect throwing away their hard earned funds (usually saved from their previous career) into advertising. Any form of promotion should be researched and approached in the same manner you would use with your therapy clients.

Advertising is not marketing but is just one part of the process. Marketing involves the four Ps: Product (or service), Promotion, Price and Place. Each has an important role to play. Get any one of them wrong and you will lose business. To the four Ps we should add a fifth P: Persistence. Persistence pays dividends.

The purpose of this book is to give you so many ways of

marketing your practice that it would be virtually impossible to fail. Yet, even armed with this book some will still not see the light. A history teacher whose students were worried about a forthcoming exam was heard to say that even if she gave them all the questions, there would be some students who would still fail. Her message was simple: having the information to succeed is one thing, using it is another. If you want to succeed you need to take action again and again.

If you use this book as it is intended you should be able to create a tidal wave of enquiries from potential clients. Take the ideas detailed here and not only use them as they stand but also adapt them to your circumstances. When you have undertaken all the marketing methods in this book you will be ready to start from the beginning again. There are many more than 101 ways to market your practice. You will know that you are successful when you start to create your own ideas.

Look at it this way: if you just manage to attract one extra client through reading this book, it will have paid for itself. In reality this book has the potential to pay for itself over and over again.

1

Practice Places

Where you decide to practise your therapy from can enhance or detract from your ability to attract clients. Some successful therapists practise from more than one venue.

1 YOUR HOME

Many therapists start a practice from their home. The home provides a number of advantages for the new or experienced therapist as long as you live in a convenient location for your clients. There are also disadvantages.

Advantages

- No extra rental costs are involved for the use of a room at home.

- No long-term contract commitments.

- The home offers a degree of anonymity to your client.

- It's more comfortable and relaxed in your own home.

- More flexibility about when you see your clients.

- No time lost travelling and no transport costs.

Disadvantages

- Disruption to the rest of your family.

- Clients may query your professionalism.

- Maintenance of parts of your home to clinical standards.

- Inconvenience of having a room that may need to be rearranged every day between family and therapy use.

- You may not be able to offer a separate waiting room.

Your local council will not have any objections to you running a therapy business from home as long as the external appearance of your residence is not altered and the running of the business does not upset neighbours. A mortgage lender may want you to take out a different insurance policy if they become aware that you work from home.

Essential home preparations

From the first moment a new client sees your home they are going to be judging you. They will be looking at your privet hedge or the lawn of your front garden. If they are neat and tidy, they will start to piece together a favourable impression of your home and you. If the garden is a complete eyesore, they will start to have second thoughts. Once someone starts to formulate an opinion they look for more evidence to support that opinion. If they then spot yellowish net curtains and a window that has been patched up with cardboard, don't expect them to come back!

We are all guilty of getting used to how our home looks, good or bad. We have seen that bare patch of wall so many times that our mind no longer registers its significance. A great way of finding out how your property is viewed through the eyes of a client is to get a friend to pretend to be a client. Get them to approach your home as though they were seeing it for the first time. Encourage them to be honest. Once you have a list of areas that could be improved, it is down to you whether to change them or not.

The survey by your friend should continue past the front door and you should greet them like a prospective client. Guide them all the way through the hallway into your treatment room and talk to them as though they have arrived for their first therapy session. Your friend should not only keep their eyes peeled for matters that are not so pleasant but in doing so utilise the other four senses: smell, taste, hearing and touch.

The treatment room

Not everyone will have the luxury of owning a room whose sole purpose will be for therapy. From a tax (capital gains) perspective it is better if the room has a dual purpose. You may have to opt to use one of the busiest rooms in the house, such as the living room. This will restrict members of the family to certain areas of the home when you are treating a client. Your family will have to be discreet, curtail some of their usual activities and keep noise to a minimum. Doors to other rooms will need to be closed for privacy and your family will need to avoid meeting your client in the hallway or on the way to the toilet. Also be aware of any cooking odours.

Clients will probably be happy about seeing personal items in a room because this helps them to formulate an idea of your personality and interests. If you have a client seeking help with problems in their family, they will feel that you are likely to be more empathetic if they see a family photograph in the room. Alternatively, this might work against you if your client is single and has a perception that you do not view the world as they do. These indications of your personal life can be helpful, unhelpful or neutral, so look around your room and imagine how your clients will react to it.

You may have to go to the inconvenience of constantly rearranging the practice room for your first client and then when you are finished for the day having to put the room back to its original order. You will need to consider where will you store therapy items (couches, towels, oils, electronic equipment, etc.) in between practice times and you will require a secure filing system for your client records. Your clients will want to be assured that their details will remain confidential. If you maintain client records you will need to comply with the Data Protection

Act (details of the regulations can be found at your local library).

If you are unable to use a room on the ground floor then you have the concern that a particular client may have great difficulty negotiating stairs. A ground floor treatment room and upstairs toilet present a similar problem.

Building rapport

Build rapport quickly. Your client is coming to a strange building (your home) to meet a person they have only ever spoken to on the telephone. The first few moments of meeting someone are very significant if the relationship is going to work.

When they knock at the door, unless you have a receptionist, it should be you, the therapist who greets them. Do not send one of your children to answer the door as your professional status will plummet.

Your first words should be precise, clear and yet friendly. Repeat the client's name and introduce yourself with a firm handshake. For example, 'Hello David, my name is Susan Blake. I am the kinesiologist'. In the space of a few seconds you have achieved a number of important things. You have confirmed to the client that they were expected and have come to the right address. You have confirmed your name and that you are the therapist. You have assured them that you are in control. Clients want to feel that you know what you are doing. This positive welcome gets you off to a great start.

When they get to the treatment room make sure that they have a good look around before you close the door to the room. Do not be in any hurry to shut them in. Building rapport varies from person to person and therapy to therapy. Some practitioners will offer the client a cup of coffee or tea or a glass of water at this point. If they accept, from a psychological point of view it can be quite significant. It shows they are willing to accept something from you and can also help them to relax more in your company. The subconscious mind will remember an association between tea or coffee and a nice comfortable chat with friends or family.

Some therapists do not offer refreshments but prefer to keep matters on a business-like level. There are pros and cons with either approach. You should decide which one you are happy with. Of course the drink may delay matters or may not be appropriate prior to the therapy you offer. Time may also be a factor. If you have to wait 15 minutes for your client to finish their herbal tea before you can massage them, your next session will be delayed.

Safety at home

There are security risks posed by having a stranger in your home: risks to your personal safety and to your property.

If you have other family members in the home when clients call then you will feel a lot safer. All new clients are strangers until you get to know them and form that professional relationship. Your clients will want to feel safe and secure with you and the building they are visiting for treatment. If they know or sense that they are not alone with you in the home, they will generally feel safer and more relaxed. This is particularly true of a male therapist and female client and vice versa, but not exclusively.

Keep a mobile telephone handy with a telephone number pre-programmed. This can be a useful way of letting a relative, friend or neighbour know you need help. After some experience most therapists are able to tell from the first telephone call whether they should agree to see a new client or not. If you are not sure and do agree to see a client it would be wise to let someone know that you may need their intervention. Knowing you have this arrangement can help you to relax more. There is nothing worse than the therapist being more nervous than the client!

Working from home can be just as successful as from a clinic as long as you have taken into account all the factors involved.

19

2 A COMPLEMENTARY THERAPY CENTRE OR CLINIC

For many reasons you may decide that to practise from home is not appropriate. You may conclude that it would be best to work some days from home and others from a therapy centre or clinic. For the therapist, this is a popular option.

Advantages

- You'll have a room specifically for therapy.
- There is no inconvenience to your family.
- There is a receptionist to take your bookings.
- There is a waiting room for clients who arrive early.
- Clients may be able to pay for treatment using credit cards.
- Networking with other therapists working there will reduce your feeling of isolation.
- Working at the clinic gives a greater sense of professionalism.
- Your may receive referrals from other fellow therapists who use the centre.
- Your can share advertising costs.
- Personal safety may be improved.
- A quiet environment.

Disadvantages

- There are extra costs involved in paying for the room.
- You can only see clients when the room is available.
- Travelling time to the therapy centre and transport costs.

- The environment may be too clinical and stark for the client.
- The clinic's location on a busy high street may reduce anonymity.

Deciding where to practise

To help you decide whether a particular therapy centre is appropriate, take a friend or relative with you when you visit for the first time to act as an extra pair of eyes. It is amazing what you, the therapist, can overlook when getting caught up in the excitement of visualising yourself in full practice. A level-headed friend can point this out to you.

Take into account accessibility for certain types of clients. Not all clients will have their own means of transport and may rely on trains or buses to get about. Check how frequently they run and how close these facilities are to your intended practice. Find out about the train and bus timetables because your clients will expect you to have this information and you will want to make it easy for them to see you. Also locate where the nearest car parks or restriction-free streets are. Poor transport communications can hamper the growth of your practice. You also need to check that the building has adequate facilities for a person with a disability.

Generally, a room in a therapy health centre will come ready for your immediate use. You pay for a room that is pleasant, clean and fresh. The adjacent rooms will be used by other therapists who respect the need for confidentiality and control of noise.

You won't have to concern yourself with family members trudging around the house or the sound of stereos, televisions or radios being on too loud. There will be no pets to control or cooking smells to mask. Access for people with a disability should also be better.

Usually, the clinic will have a central reception and waiting area, all adding to the air of professionalism. The receptionist will take bookings for you and greet your clients when they arrive for their appointment to see you. The clinic will have (by law) a suitable number of toilets that will be cleaned and freshened on a regular basis. Some clinics also provide showers for clients.

Good clinics also consider the smaller touches which make a real difference. They may provide boxes of tissues in each room, fresh flowers, water coolers and coffee and tea making facilities. The receptionist may even offer to make coffee or tea for your client before the appointment starts. All of these extras add an air of welcome to your clients and will help with word-of-mouth marketing.

Costs and payments

The clinic may offer an arrangement for the client to pay the clinic directly. You get reimbursed for your client fees (less the room rent) at the end of the week. This can be useful when your client wants to pay by credit card. It is far more economical and logical for the clinic to deal with credit card transactions rather than an individual therapist.

You will be expected to hire a room in blocks of four or five hours each week. Whether you have clients during all, part of or none of these hours, you will still be charged for the room. The best times are from five o'clock in the evening on weekdays. This is the time that most people will have finished work and be available for therapy. Saturdays are also popular with clients for the same reason.

If you are unable to secure these times then think twice about operating from that clinic or negotiate a better deal for the less popular times. You may even be able to persuade the clinic to give you floating times that you use on an hour by hour basis and pay for only when you have a client.

The treatment room

No room is ever ideal and so you will need to be able to see the potential. You can add to a room's feel and ambience but you should not have to bring in large items of furniture. You can add a cushion, pillow or throw if you want to add to the cosiness or you may decide that simple and clinical is better. Either way, you can completely change the feel of a place by using your creativity and moving furniture around or adding little extras. You need to be as comfortable in your surroundings as your client is going to be.

You can enhance the room by adding some personal touch of your own. This can be something as simple as a favourite essential oil in an oil burner or fresh flowers.

Building rapport

When your new client comes for their first appointment this is most likely the first time that they will have had any contact with you. They will generally only have had contact with the receptionist and so will only know your name and some of your details. If you practise from home, you would have spoken to the new client on the telephone and the important factor of building a working relationship would already have begun.

They say first impressions count, so here is your chance to make or break the relationship in the first minutes. Consciously or subconsciously, you are being assessed by your client from the very first point of contact. So be confident, be focussed and know what you are doing. Make some 'small talk' with the client as you guide them to the treatment room.

Once the client is in the room be concerned about their comfort and give an outline of the immediate session. If this is an assessment session, tell them this again and the choices that they will have at the end of it. The more you keep your client informed, the more comfortable they will feel, and nothing will surprise them.

Safety at the clinic

Your own safety should be enhanced at a clinic for the simple reason that there are always people coming and going. Even if you are the only therapist working in the evening, there should always be another person in the building such as the receptionist or the person responsible for closing up at night.

Fellow therapists

You will gradually meet the other therapists working at the clinic. This is a great opportunity for gaining referrals and exchanging therapies. Working at the centre can help to reduce the isolation often felt by people who have changed from an employed status and working with others, to self-employed and working alone. The cost of advertising can also be shared among the therapists and the therapy centre.

3 RENTING A ROOM

Practising from a rented room in a building that is not a 'designated' clinic or therapy centre has the potential to be as successful as any other option. Many aspects are similar to renting a room in a clinic. However, there are other issues that need to be taken into account.

Advantages

- Rental costs (pro rata) are significantly less than in a therapy centre or clinic.

- You'll have sole use of the room.

- There are more options with regard to the location of your practice.

- You will enjoy networking opportunities with neighbouring businesses.

Disadvantages

- You will incur costs of bringing the room to an acceptable standard.

- There is lack of control over noise from neighbouring businesses.

- The building may lack reception facilities.

- You will need to take into account travelling time to the building and transport costs.

Surveying the room and building

Assuming you are renting the room for a minimum of six months and that you are the only user of the room, you may get a completely empty room, in which case you can furnish it exactly the way you want. Usually you will not find any objection from the owners if you want to improve the decoration of the room. It can be quite a bonus to have a blank canvas and be able to create a room with your own personal touches.

Unfortunately, there is a possibility that this room may have neighbours whose businesses can be noisy or, through the nature of their business reflect badly on you. It is imperative that you find out who your neighbours are. You will not want to achieve complete silence but will need a room that is not going to be disturbed by excessive noise, smells or other environmental factors.

As the sole occupant of the room you will be responsible for keeping it in a usable and acceptable condition to your clients. Therefore you will need to clean and maintain the facilities within the room. The hallway leading to the rooms will generally be the responsibility of the building management and you should be aware of their arrangements regarding the maintenance of this area.

You may also find it necessary to provide refreshments for your clients such as water from a dispenser or hot drinks. The provision of this and other minor details is down to your own personal taste. It is worth noting that paying attention to small details like this can really make a difference to how your clients feel about the quality of service you provide.

The building may still have a receptionist or security guard but they will not be as welcoming as a receptionist in a clinic. You may wish to make an arrangement with the receptionist that your clients are either directed to your room or asked to wait in the reception area for you to meet and greet them. Trial and error will, as always, teach you the best way to operate.

Once you have committed yourself to renting or leasing a room in a multi-purpose building it is a good idea to get to know your neighbours. Make friends with them and they will be more likely to co-operate should you need to ask for anything. This is an opportunity to network and you may be surprised how many clients are referred to you from the businesses in the same building if you take the trouble to build good relationships with them.

4 MOBILE THERAPY

The more options you can offer a client, the more you are likely to satisfy their needs and circumvent any objections. Objections are reasons that potential customers have for not making a buying decision. Offering a mobile form of your therapy can be a way of reaching those clients who for various reasons cannot get to you. These might be mothers who cannot leave their home because of their children; it could be older people who have no transport and cannot negotiate public transport; it could be someone who suffers from a phobia about cars, tubes and trains or even agoraphobia (fear of open spaces).

Advantages

- There are no rental costs.
- There is no disruption to the family home.
- You will not have any lease or rent contract commitments.
- The client will be more relaxed in their own home.

Disadvantages

- You will be practising in a strange environment.
- There is the uncertainty of available facilities.
- You will incur extra transport costs and lose time travelling to and from appointments.
- You will have to transport your therapy equipment.

Structuring your fees

As a mobile therapist, what you save on room rent costs, you lose on transport costs and your time in travelling to the client's home. All these factors should be taken into account when deciding your fee structure. People are willing to pay a higher price for the convenience of having the service come to them. Include an additional amount for the travelling time and costs in your therapy fees.

Many newly qualified therapists, who initially have no place from which to practise, start off their business by visiting clients in their homes. Once they are established they tend to drop the mobile option from their service, yet it can be a useful extra, particularly if no-one else is offering it.

Taking control of your practice

The drawback of offering a mobile service is that you are not in as much control as you would like to be. You are reliant on your client being able to provide some of the facilities needed for your therapy – aspects like a quiet and private room, a comfortable armchair and wash facilities. There may be an occasion when your client is not at home when you arrive for the appointment. There is nothing more annoying then travelling to see someone who is not in when you arrive.

Given enough thought, many of these situations can be eased or avoided altogether. Emphasise with any client the minimum facilities that you must have at their home. You might ask them to pay for their session in advance to cover for the possibility of them not keeping the appointment.

Mobile therapy can work very well for any therapist as long as you consider all the different dimensions of operating this way.

5 BUYING AN EXISTING PRACTICE

Just like any other commercial concern, you can get the opportunity to buy another person's practice. The word 'practice' can mean many things. It could mean the whole building, existing clients (private and corporate) and past clients and any current employees plus ongoing arrangements and agreements (including advertising). It could also simply mean the existing clients. It is not the purpose of this chapter to go into all the intricacies of purchasing an existing business but to point out some of the advantages and disadvantages. You should always seek professional advice on any major purchase of this nature.

Advantages

- You will have an immediate client base.
- You are taking over an established business.
- Set procedures and systems will be in place.
- Goodwill can help you to get off to a flying start.

Disdavantages

- You will have the initial purchase expense.
- Existing clients may change to another therapist.

If everything goes well, purchasing an existing practice means that you are up and running immediately. With goodwill included, the vendor should have made clear the strategies that work for this practice, so you have systems and procedures in place and an existing client base. If the business has been successful and you repeat those past strategies, then logically you should be able to continue that success. One of the biggest assets should be that the practice is well known because it has been in business for some time.

On the other hand, how successful is the practice really?

- Why is the person selling the business?

- Will all the clients be happy to see a new therapist or will they take this opportunity to stop their therapy or seek out a different therapist?

- Will past clients object to you contacting them?

- If the practice is known by the (selling) therapist's name, will you be able to trade using that name even though they no longer work at the practice?

As long as you have weighed up all these considerations, then there is no reason why purchasing an existing practice at the right price cannot be a success and get you over the hurdles of starting a brand new practice.

6 HEALTH SUITES IN SPORTS CENTRES

Major sports centres provide additional services often under the umbrella of the 'Beauty and Health Suite'. These regular services can be facials, manicures and pedicures and hair styling. The facilities in these suites may be appropriate for your type of therapy.

Very few health suites will be fully booked throughout the week. The management of the suite will be interested in offering other complementary services to the public to fill those empty slots. If you can offer a service which is not currently being provided and the facilities they have (massage couch, private cubicle, washing facilities, etc.) are appropriate for your therapy, you may find an additional place to ply your trade.

A convenient arrangement is to agree a set time and day that you would see your clients at the centre. The centre will normally take responsibility for attracting clients and giving them appointment times. Their general marketing programme can now include the service you offer. The responsibility for getting clients would be the centre's and not yours. For this reason it is important to obtain an understanding that you only pay for rental of the space or room when you have a client booked. If you don't have a client then you don't pay for the time and the room can be used by another therapist.

The usefulness of this idea is that you do not have to concern yourself with marketing your services because the centre will have its own blanket advertising strategy. Successful therapists assist this by providing leaflets and posters.

7 PRIVATE HEALTH CLUBS

In an effort to attract as many clients as possible, private health clubs and health farms are offering as many therapies as possible. In the old days it used to be a gym, with a fitness regime, maybe a diet to follow and a sauna and steam room. Today, any process or service that can enhance a customer's feel good factor will be added to the range on offer. The larger the range of services, the more likely that a customer is going to find what they like and what works for them.

Complementary and alternative therapies are being added to many health resorts' menus. A massage service has nearly always been available but now you can get aromatherapy, osteopathy, Alexander technique, yoga and much more. With this in mind, you can form an agreement with these places and enjoy a steady flow of clients.

Some health clubs will take responsibility for marketing your therapy and book in clients for you on a set day and at a set time. Others will take more of a back seat and expect you to provide leaflets and posters and make yourself available to promote your service.

Costs to therapists vary. Some places will charge rent for a room and others will take a percentage of your fee. Make sure you know in advance which system is going to operate as you may need to increase your usual fees. Generally, you will be allocated a set number of hours on an agreed day each week. This makes matters easier, as knowing when you will offer your therapy at the club will enable you to arrange your private clients at other times.

Your initial approach to health clubs or resorts is best done by telephone. There is no point in writing a letter to a place that doesn't have the room or has someone else offering your therapy already. Phoning also gives you the opportunity to find out the name of the person to contact. You might be invited to have a look around immediately but if not, follow up your telephone call with a letter. Include the benefits of your therapy to their clients and how well it has been received in other places (if you can, give examples). State the bare minimum of facilities you would require. After a week follow the letter up with another telephone call to the named contact while the matter is still fresh in their mind. You can approach a private gymnasium in a similar way.

8 WORKING AS A CORPORATE ON-SITE THERAPIST

Large corporations have many facilities which are often under-utilised. Instead of offering a group workshop or course to a large company you could try offering to be an 'on-site' therapist. This type of employee benefit is becoming more and more popular.

Advantages

- There are no marketing costs.
- The company informs all employees about your services.
- There is the possible provision of a room without costs.
- Your reputation can spread like wild fire, particularly in an office or factory environment.
- Employees may also want to see you at your own private practice.
- Clients may recommend your therapy to friends, relatives and acquaintances.

Disadvantages

- Clients may not feel so comfortable seeking treatment while at work.

- Clients may be concerned about confidentiality.

Generally, the company provides private rooms and the necessary equipment in the room and then invites therapists to provide services such as autogenic training, homeopathy, reflexology and Indian head massage to name a few. Under the rules of the benefit, the employees may either make a contribution towards the service or the company may pay all of the individual fees. Usually, the company just provides the facilities and the employee pays for the therapy that they undergo.

The benefits for the therapist are that you have a captive audience. You will have no marketing costs, as the company informs all employees that the service exists. You normally won't have any rent costs because the company provides the rooms. Your reputation can spread through word-of-mouth recommendations. You may also get employees preferring to see you in your own private practice away from prying eyes.

9 DOCTORS' SURGERIES

A great place to base your practice, even if it is only part time, is at a doctor's surgery. Many surgeries have spare rooms and it is a way for them to gain extra funds. Not all doctors will agree to this. It really comes down to how informed your local doctor is and their opinion on your therapy.

Advantages

- You will receive referrals from the GPs in the practice.

- There is an increased public perception of quality and professionalism.

- Your therapy moves closer to being more widely accepted by the orthodox medical profession.
- You will have reduced marketing costs.

Disadvantages

- You will incur the extra costs involved in paying for the room.
- You can only see clients within the surgery opening times.
- You will have to take into account travelling time to the surgery and transport costs.
- The environment may be too clinical and stark for the client.
- The surgery management may restrict the ailments you can treat.

More and more therapists are securing rooms at surgeries. It is a great way to build a bridge between conventional and complementary medicine. In building better relations and because of the close proximity, you will start to receive referrals from the doctors who practise there. They will mostly be private patients but they will be referrals none-the-less.

In the waiting area you have a captive audience and practice managers will be more receptive to you leaving your leaflets in this area. Some therapists who secure a place at a doctor's surgery find that they can really cut down on their other marketing strategies.

Whether you practise full or part time from a doctor's surgery it will add an important dimension to your service: quality. Clients will assume that you must be good in order to be able to base yourself there. Perceptions count for a lot in any business.

2

Practice Management

Pay attention to the small details of running a practice and you increase your chances of growing and maintaining a smooth and professional operation.

(10) DECIDING WHAT TO CHARGE

Many new therapists stumble over how much to charge clients. The answer is to charge what you are worth. If you value what you provide, the client will value it too.

Deciding your value

Telephone the competition in your area to find out what their fees are for the service they provide. It is important to find out this information from a therapist who provides the same therapy as you. You need to compare like with like.

You will get a mix of prices and services. One therapist may charge £45 for an hour's therapy and give a free 15-minute consultation. Another will charge £75 for the first session, give a free 30-minute consultation, and then charge £55 for subsequent sessions. The idea of doing a survey of the competition is to gauge the range of fees that are appropriate to your location and therapy.

You do not have to keep within the range of fees you discover from your research, it is merely for you to make an informed decision about where to set your fees. The cost of therapy is a big part of the decision making process for any potential client. Set your fees too low and they will think that your service lacks quality, that you don't have much experience or you are desperate for their business. You may start to begrudge the time you give your client and this is not a resourceful state to be in. Set your fees too high and you will be outside many clients' affordability range. It is far better to find a fee that respects your value, is affordable to the majority of enquirers and has taken into account your expenses. Remember that your expenses might include:

- heat
- light
- rent
- travel
- products
- equipment
- insurance
- professional fees.

Concessions

Some therapists offer a sliding scale of fees and a reduced fee to those who are unemployed, on low incomes or, for acceptable reasons, are unable to afford your full fee. Others believe that they should not reduce their fees. Indeed some would say that clients who are not punctual, do not carry out agreed tasks between sessions, or who simply do not keep their appointments often seem to be those who have been granted a reduced fee. It could be argued that a reduced fee brings with it a perception of lower value and a lack of motivation from the client.

If you give a reduction in your fees get the client to agree to see you during less popular times during the day. Prime times such as evenings and weekends should be the preserve of those who will pay your full fee.

Your practice rules

Clearly explain your practice rules to your clients. If you require 24 hours' notice of a cancellation, tell them. Let them know in advance what would be the forfeit if they do not follow this rule. If they give you less than 24 hours' notice the charge would be 50% of your fee, for example. Less than 12 hours' notice and the full fee may be due.

If you accept telephone bookings you can state your fees and cancellation policy and follow this up in writing as a way of confirming the appointment. Some therapists charge for one session in advance. This encourages the client to attend the appointment or to give you adequate notice that they can't make the time and date.

Your fee structure and rules of business should be made known to your client as soon as possible and then the chance of misunderstandings occurring will be reduced.

Lastly, you should review your fees at least annually to take into account changing circumstances and inflation.

11 MAKING IT EASY TO BUY

It would be a pity if having attended many different therapy courses, read numerous therapy books, undergone examinations and joined appropriate associations, you fell at the final hurdle. Once a customer has made a decision to buy your service, you should make it as easy as possible for them to achieve that purchase.

Opening hours

Are your hours flexible enough for your clients? You will lose a potential client if you cannot find a convenient time. Most people will have a daytime occupation and will not be able to accept a daytime appointment. Your evening appointments will be very popular and at times these may be booked two or three weeks ahead, even though you still have plenty of daytime slots left.

If this pattern continues you may lose people who want to see you in a reasonable amount of time but are unable to because the nearest appointment you can give them is a month away. You should then consider whether to be available for some hours at the weekend. Many therapists have a Saturday morning clinic that takes the pressure off their evening times. Other therapists pick one day in the week when they will not see clients and then make themselves available for the whole of Saturday. The appointment times on Saturday should be the preserve of those who cannot make any other time. Use it as a fall back position only if you are unable to agree a convenient appointment time during the weekdays with a client.

At the commencement of any new practice you may need to accept bookings at odd and often inconvenient times. When you get busier, you can start to be more selective about the hours that you make yourself available.

Payment
The client has had their therapy session and now the time has come for them to pay your fee. The easiest payment method for the therapist is cash. After that the next easiest payment method is a cheque with a banker's guarantee card. How will you handle the situation if the client is expecting to be able to pay by credit card? If you can't accept credit cards and the client does not have enough cash or a cheque book with them, what will you do?

To avoid the above embarrassing situation you have two options. You can either tell the client, in advance that you can't except credit card payments (and risk the loss of business) or you can take steps to arrange to accept credit cards. The cost of accepting payment this way will be a percentage of your fee to the credit card company. Some companies require you to make a payment for any equipment needed to process a credit card transaction. New therapists can operate quite successfully without accepting credit card payments. As you become busier and your fee increases you may find that a credit card facility is a necessity. In fact some clients may not take you seriously if you don't accept credit cards.

Location
If you are not sure of how to get to your practice from other locations, how do you expect your clients to arrive

there on time? Acquaint yourself with all the forms of transport that can help someone to find your practice easily and effortlessly. Memorise bus numbers and train timetables. Familiarise yourself with different routes so that you can give directions to anyone travelling by car. Go over the directions you give out and make them as 'idiot proof' as you can.

If at all possible try to send directions by email, fax or letter. The more you assist your client's journey the greater their chances of arriving on time, and in a good state of mind. Just try having a therapy session with someone who is 30 minutes late and flustered – and you can only give them 45 minutes because of your next appointment. Help your clients and you will help your practice to run smoothly.

12 CONVERTING ENQUIRIES INTO CLIENTS

Getting the client to telephone, write to or email you is the first step in the marketing process. The subsequent steps of responding to their communication must be good enough to convert them into a paying client.

Some enquirers have made up their mind and will simply want to book a session without needing to ask questions. Others will ask from one to a dozen questions before they will make a decision. Remember that as long as they ask questions, they are interested. Answer their questions and reassure them and you will get another appointment time filled.

Answering questions successfully

Most of the questions asked by enquirers you will have heard before, and you should have tried and tested answers. On a website there will often be a page dedicated to FAQs or 'Frequently Asked Questions' for this very reason. Some questions may surprise you. If this happens don't blurt out some waffle. Take your time in responding. Use the old tactic of repeating the question back to the caller, which will give you more time to think about the answer. Never lie or make promises that you cannot deliver. If you genuinely cannot answer a question say so. They will have more belief in you because of your honesty.

Organisations often use telesales teams who are given a script to read to customers. This provides a uniform standard of customer communication across the company. Although your response should not be rigid, memorising a standard response will be helpful. It gives you more confidence and it sounds to the client you know what you are talking about.

Communicating the session fees

If a client asks you how much a session costs, do not blurt out the price straightaway. Say to them, 'Can I tell you what is involved in a session so that you know what you are paying for?' This gives you control: you can outline the benefits of your service before mentioning your charges. Tell them what a session involves and include any extras such as a free consultation. At the end say something like 'and your investment in your health is £50'. But do not let the '£50' float around in their mind. After informing them of the cost, immediately ask them 'Do you have any other questions I can help you with?' If you do this they are not left with £50 stuck in their mind but are thinking if they need any other information.

Prepare set responses

If you get an enquiry by email, have some prepared responses ready. This saves a lot of time and also ensures you don't forget any important details. You can always personalise your response by including their name and answering specific questions not covered in your standard reply. The same procedure is applicable to writing letters to potential clients. Always enclose your practice brochure when corresponding by letter.

TALKING TO CLIENTS ON THE TELEPHONE

Your marketing effort continues with the telephone. If you can have a dedicated telephone line just for your therapy practice, so much the better. This way you will always know that when the telephone rings it will be a business call and you can answer it in a professional manner. Other members of the family will also know to leave the telephone for you to answer or to take a message in an appropriate way.

Handling calls when you are busy

Potential clients may telephone you when you are in a therapy session, are out elsewhere or when you are using the telephone. To cover for this eventuality some therapists use a telephone bureau. The bureau takes your calls for you in a professional manner. The potential client always gets to talk to a person as opposed to a machine. The bureaux will also book clients for you if you provide them with the information about how to handle your calls. There is a charge for this service that on average is about £50 per month. If your fees are £50 and you receive one extra booking a month through using this service (that you may have otherwise lost) it will pay for itself.

If you decide that the telephone bureau is not appropriate, for whatever reason, invest in an answering machine or service. Many telephone companies provide an answering service and will record a message (even if you are using the telephone at the time) rather than just give the caller an engaged tone. If the caller cannot contact you, then the next best option is an answering machine or service. If they just get no answer, they may give up and seek out another therapist.

When you pick up your telephone messages, you must telephone the client back as soon as you can. Even though they have left you a message and contact number, that doesn't mean that they are going to wait for you to telephone back. Some clients ring around a number of

therapists and will book an appointment with the first
therapist they speak to.

Not all clients will want to leave a message, and another
useful facility is a redirection service. All calls from your
business telephone can be re-routed through to your
mobile or other telephone by punching in a special code.
If you are available to take those calls this is an excellent
way of not missing any potential clients.

Easy to remember

Your telephone number can also help your marketing. You
can purchase personal numbers that equate to words or
form memorable numbers. It is much easier for a client to
remember 07777 29 29 29 than 060 7967 29783. Memorable
numbers are particularly useful with a radio marketing
campaign.

(14) OFFERING A FREE PHONE NUMBER

You can encourage potential clients to contact you by
making a free telephone service available. This can
sometimes make the difference between someone taking
action or not. It gives the added incentive that by
telephoning you for more information they are not losing
anything because the telephone call is free.

Advantages

If you are able to boast a free phone number it does
enhance your public persona. It gives the impression that
this business takes itself seriously, is professional and will
be around for sometime. A free phone number also deals
with a small objection that some people may have – i.e. the
cost of the call.

You can enhance your 'pulling power' even further if
you manage to obtain a free phone number that is
memorable.

Increased costs

The negative side of a free phone number is that your
business pays for the customer's call and there is an
additional service charge on top of this. You might also
wonder, if a person is unwilling to spend a few pennies on
a telephone call, how will they cope when you tell them
your therapy fees? Some existing customers may take
advantage of the free phone by using it for purposes such
as cancelling appointments, rearrangements and general
queries.

In order to keep your costs under control you will need
to make it clear that existing customers must use a
different telephone number. You can achieve this by
calling the free phone number an 'information' line and
emphasizing that its use is only for new clients who are
considering therapy.

(15) RETAINING CLIENTS

Having attracted a client to your practice through one of
your many marketing ideas, now is not the time to lose the
plot. Everything you do with this client from the first
telephone call to the last goodbye, must ooze quality and
professionalism.

Help clients relax quickly

You can help clients to relax by building rapport quickly,
but don't get over friendly. There is a fine line between
keeping the interaction jovial and warm and stepping over
the line into treating the client like a buddy. They are the
'customer' and you are the 'provider' of a service. They
want the best for their money. If you let your professional
persona drop during the session, there is the possibility
that you will lose your concentration and become sloppy.

Listen to your clients

If you have an unhappy client do not reach for the book of
excuses, just listen to them. They want to know that you

have understood why they are unhappy. If you feel the client has a genuine complaint, then take action to make amends. If they don't have a good reason for a complaint then you need to be firm in explaining your point of view.

For every single unhappy client who expresses their disappointment, research has shown that there are at least another six in existence who have been unhappy but have not said anything to you. These clients will never come back to you but they may tell others about their dissatisfaction. The one client who has complained has actually done you a favour. They have pointed out a problem and if you correct it, this can save you losing many more clients. When you look at it this way, you can see that it is well worth your while making the effort and meeting the expense of regaining the good will of that unhappy client.

Often, if you make amends, the client who complained can become your best referral source. You have made them feel valued and cared about their issues, and this can really transform how someone feels about you and your therapy.

16 SPECIALISING

If you had a particular ailment and you wanted to see a therapist for help, you would want to know that the therapist had expertise or at least some experience in that area. It really can pay huge dividends for you to have a more in-depth knowledge of a particular ailment and the techniques to help.

Often an area of specialisation selects you. For some reason therapists seem to attract certain clients and certain ailments. Sometimes you may find a niche thrust upon you. However, you can also decide that you would like to focus on people who have eczema, for example. The more you study and make this ailment your own special area, the more your therapy skills will be refined and the more people you can help.

After a time you will find that you become known as the person to see if you have eczema. This reputation not only builds amongst potential clients but also with your fellow therapists. You may even find your colleagues in the same field referring their clients with eczema to you.

Specialising does not stop you from helping the usual collection of problems but adds a new dimension to your marketing. Clients who know you have good results with one ailment will assume that you are just as successful in other areas. There is nothing quite like the reputation of an expert to help your practice keep busy through personal recommendations.

Becoming a perceived expert in a certain ailment can also help you to increase your income in other areas. You can give lectures to existing therapy schools as master classes for their therapists. You can also provide your own independently run workshops.

With more experience you will start to use the language that medical experts use to describe aspects of the ailment. In any communication with these experts or other bodies it can reassure them that you do know what you are talking about and will give you a better chance of getting the message across that you do have something worthwhile to contribute.

(17) ASSISTING RECOMMENDATIONS

When you have your client's attention, and the opportunity arises, include in the conversation examples of how you have helped other people. The best time is when you are chatting at the outset to a new client. In order to help them know that you get results, you can give anecdotal examples of your success. Also do this when they have finished their session and you are back to 'small talk' before they leave your practice. Rather than talking about the weather or how bad the traffic is, why not talk about a success story.

When the client says at the end of their therapy, 'Thanks I really enjoyed that', you can say, 'Good, but you know,

NLP never ceases to amaze me. Why only recently I helped someone who lacked confidence for years to get their life back together. They are now running their own successful business'. A hypnotherapist might say, 'Quite recently I helped someone overcome their needle phobia which used to prevent them from going to the dentist'.

These anecdotes plant a seed in the client's mind. The client might not have come for confidence or a phobia but they will eventually meet someone who has got one of these issues and they may say 'I know someone who can help you with that'.

By taking the time to mention other ailments you have successfully treated, you gain the assistance of your current client with your marketing effort. Everyone loves to feel knowledgeable and to give advice. You client gets to feel good by informing someone of a therapist who may be able to help them.

18 PROVIDING TESTIMONIALS

People feel more secure knowing that they are not the first person you have seen for a particular problem. They want to know that you have expertise and have had success in the areas with which they need help. Nothing helps with this more than having some testimonials ready to show your clients. For those clients who are undecided at the initial consultation, the production of a few testimonials can work wonders.

If you are going to show any correspondence you have received from happy clients you must have their permission, otherwise your confidentiality guarantee will be compromised. If you still want to show testimonials but don't have permission from the client, than cover up the name and address details. The easiest way to do this is to photocopy the testimonials and black out the identifying details. The reader can then see that the testimonial is real but cannot see who sent it.

Quoting testimonials

On your leaflet include a few quotes from those letters and cards, but again keep it anonymous. If you want to refer to the person, do so by their ailment.

'I was so relaxed travelling to Sydney, Australia . . .'
flying phobia

'I feel so much more in control of my life . . .'
executive stress

'The pain has gone completely . . .'   *joint pain*

You can also show these quotes from satisfied clients on your website, posters, brochures, leaflets, mini-manuals and advertisements (see Chapter 3 for more on these).

(19) PLAYING IT COOL

If you are not getting enough clients and are desperate for the telephone to ring, make sure that this does not become apparent in your manner or voice. Nothing will drive a client away faster than the impression that you don't have many clients and will do anything to encourage someone to come along. 'Anything', does not mean marketing. Doing 'anything' can mean promising the client 'the earth' when you know that you cannot or are not sure that you can help them. Another mistake is to give the impression that you have plenty of appointments available. The client will conclude that if you are available to see them at any time, you don't have many clients and must therefore be a poor therapist.

Clients gain confidence in your skills if they get the impression that you are very busy. Busy equates to being successful and having a good reputation. Always talk as if you have a full practice, even if you only see three people a week.

Your fees should be set and you should not be too

willing to compromise on price. There will always be exceptions but you should try to stick to your fee structure. If you reluctantly allow yourself to be negotiated to lower fees by a client they will have the impression that your services are not valuable and therefore not the best quality and you will feel resentful towards the client because you are not getting your full fee.

Be willing to let clients go, and recommend other forms of help if they show any doubt about visiting you. The more you show that you are willing to let them make up their own mind the more they will believe that you are the person they should see. Just as with parents of teenagers, if you try to hold on to them, they will push you away, but if you let them go, they will come back of their own accord.

The impression you aim to give to everyone is of a practice that is successful and busy. You welcome new clients but you are not desperate for their business.

3

Promotional Materials

There are some information media that are essential to getting your name known and creating the right impression.

(20) YOUR PRACTICE BROCHURE

A brochure is an important aspect of your marketing. In fact it is probably the number one item in your marketing armoury. It conveys so much about you. A business card displays a small amount of information whereas a therapist's brochure includes so much more and could persuade a client to see you.

Essential details for your brochure

- Your name
- Your contact details
  - Telephone number
  - Email address
  - Website address
- Your practice address in full or just the area you are located in
- Your qualifications
- Details of training schools (if appropriate)
- Membership of any relevant organisations
- Type(s) of therapy you offer
- Benefits of your therapy
- Ailments and problems you can help with

- Answers to frequently asked questions
- Details of sessions

Putting your brochure together

If you are not sure about style and layout, go to your local library and obtain other therapists' brochures. They will give you some ideas. Most such brochures are made up of three parts, although some therapists use two parts. A three-part brochure is simply an A4 sheet of paper, turned on its side (landscape) and folded into thirds.

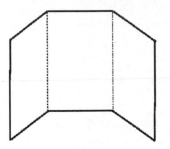 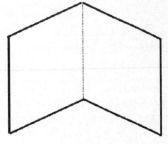

Fig. 1. Three-Part Brochure   Fig. 2. Two-Part Brochure

The front of your leaflet needs to communicate an immediate point of interest to a potential client. Ask questions and highlight benefits. Do not splash your name in the biggest typeface. Potential clients are not interested in your name, or at least not initially. They will want to know that you can help them. Use something like Figure 3.

Shy? **Nervous?** **Lack Confidence?** Do you want to boost your confidence today?	**Stressed?** **Irritable?** **Tense?** Want to learn how to relax quickly?

Fig. 3. Front Page.

49

These examples are quite specific and offer help for stress or a lack of confidence. Do not overcrowd the front page; keep it snappy and to the point. Your contact telephone number should be on the front and repeated elsewhere in the brochure. Use at least 100gsm quality paper. You may want to keep your multi-coloured brochures for this purpose. However, if you are going to distribute hundreds of brochures, then the quality can drop to 80gsm and black print on coloured paper will suffice.

It can be useful to have your marketing leaflets checked by the National Advertising Standards Authority to make sure you are not breaking advertising guidelines.

21 BUSINESS CARDS

Well-designed business cards indicate that you are serious about what you do and convey an air of respectability and professionalism. Do not go anywhere without them. You will be surprised how often you will find yourself in a situation where there is an opportunity to secure a client. Scraps of paper with your details scrawled on them will more than likely end up lost or discarded. A business card in a customer's wallet or purse will be a constant reminder of your service.

Essential details for your business card

- Your name
- Any designations
- Your profession
- Telephone numbers
- Email address
- Web site address
- Postal address

Extra details (on the back)

- A mini appointment schedule
- Rules of the practice (24 hour notice of cancellation, etc.)
- List of ailments you treat

Quality counts

Your business card must be a high-quality product. The weight of the card should be no less than 120gsm. The layout of the information must be neat, consistent and pleasant to look at. Your name, profession and telephone number will need to be in a larger typeface compared to other information.

Marketing with your business cards

Consider all the opportunities you have to offer your business card to others:

- Dropping the children off at school
- Doing the weekly grocery shop
- At a football match
- Attending a reunion of old schools chums
- At a family gathering

Keep a supply in your wallet, purse or handbag, in any jackets and in the glove compartment of the car. Give your spouse or partner a supply because they may be asked for one. In other words, never miss an opportunity to distribute your business cards.

(22) LEAFLETING

This is an area that seems so obvious, yet many people don't even consider it. One of the reasons is that the majority of leaflets pushed through letter boxes get thrown away. You have only a few seconds to grab someone's attention, as per the AIDA principles referred to in Chapter 6 under 'Newspapers'.

Numbers count

To be successful with this marketing tool you need to deliver several thousand leaflets as a minimum. It can work for you, but you need to consider whether this is an appropriate medium for the image you are trying to project. It will not appeal to all types of therapy. A counsellor may decide that this type of promotion does not reflect well on their service but a chiropractor may find it appropriate and effective.

Designing your leaflet

An A5 size leaflet is big enough to be noticed and include all the relevant details and is less expensive than an A4 leaflet. Choose a colour of paper that you feel reflects the message you are trying to get across. Do not choose bright pinks or florescent colours. Black or dark blue ink makes the typeface easy to read. Emphasise the benefits and consider including a discount coupon with a 'use by' date. Make it easy for clients to contact you.

Now add up the total costs of producing and distributing the leaflets. If you divide this total cost figure by your client fee, you get an idea of how many clients you need to attract in order to break even. Generally, you could expect a response of about a quarter to a half of one percent. For every thousand leaflets delivered, you could expect between two and five clients.

Of course, those two clients might attend for three sessions and recommend you to their friends. These are other variables to take into account when deciding if this marketing method is a winner for you or not.

SELLING THERAPY PRODUCTS

Most therapies will use items that can be supportive of the therapy. These items can be sold to the general public to increase your revenue but they can also be another way of marketing yourself.

Write a book

They say that everyone has a book inside them and this is no different for the therapist. The subject of the book could be anonymous case histories, or a 'How to do it in three easy steps' manual, or your own methods of enhancing an existing therapy. Having a book published elevates your standing in the eyes of the public. There is a perception that you must be an expert in your field if you have written a book about the subject. This perception can help attract clients to your door as well as the book earning you income in its own right.

Other side products

You can also sell other products. A hypnotherapist could sell self-hypnosis tapes. An aromatherapist might sell essential oils and oil burners. If your therapy is more practical, you could market a video of aromatherapy techniques aimed at a section of the community such as couples. A massage therapist could produce a video about baby massage or make up individual combinations of massage oil for clients. All of these items give you a chance of increasing your marketing effectiveness and also your income.

All your therapy products can be listed for sale on your practice brochure and on your website. You could even have a display of these products in your practice room or if working at a clinic, in the reception area. This way you can earn an income even if you are not in the clinic. If the product is of a good quality and packaged well, you might even persuade local health shops to display and sell it for you.

Many therapists play soothing and relaxing background

music whilst seeing a client. Clients subconsciously make an association between the music played and the good feelings they get when experiencing the therapy. With this in mind, clients may ask you where they can obtain the music. You could sell CDs, cassettes and mini discs – another opportunity to add to your income.

(24) PUBLISHING YOUR OWN NEWSLETTER

With the advent of easier and cheaper ways of producing documents to a professional standard, it is quite feasible to produce your very own newsletter. The idea of the newsletter is ultimately to promote your practice and to bring more clients to your door. However, it needs to offer a community information service.

Suitable newsletter contents

- Topical and supportive stories paraphrased from national newspapers or magazines (be aware of copyright infringements)

- Informative articles about your therapy
  – history
  – development

- Competitions

- Workshop details

- Advertising

- A list and descriptions of your therapy products

- Your contact details

- An appropriate name for the newsletter (e.g *Utopia, Tranquillity Times*, etc.)

The newsletter should include articles of an informative nature and should not be a purely promotional document. Libraries and health shops will not take any literature that is just sales material unless, in the case of a health shop, it is promoting an item they are selling.

Strike a balance between information and promotion. Have articles that talk about the causes of stress and give the top ten tips for reducing stress. One of the tips might be to take up a relaxation practice. If you are a yoga teacher, then mention yoga as a stress buster. If you are a life coach, describe how your skills can help to identify the causes of procrastination and to reduce or eliminate them.

Newsletters tend to take advertisements to help with the costs of production. You can legitimately place a reasonable number of ads in the newsletter. Just ensure that they are not in direct competition with you.

Ideally, the newsletter should be at least a B3 size but folded in half to form a booklet of A4 size. This is large enough to allow space for interesting articles, to take advertising and to include details of your treatments, courses and any workshops. Choose quality coloured paper (at least 100gsm) and colours like cream, light blues or greens. Incorporate some pictures or diagrams to break up the text and add interest.

25 MINI-MANUALS

Producing a mini-manual about your therapy is a way of guiding the novice through the basics. The manual can be similar to the classic publications, 'How to play Golf in three easy stages', ' The Lazy Man's Guide to Gardening' or 'How to give a Best Man's Speech'.

A mini-manual can be sold at fairs, via mail shots for a small fee or it can be given away to increase your client numbers. It can act like the bait on a fishing line. A small fish is used to attract and reel in a bigger fish. A mini-manual should not go into fine detail. It should just describe the basic process and may incorporate diagrams to make it an easy read – something that someone could read in an hour perhaps and get a better idea of how they can use the therapy.

The manual should include details of what can be expected from undergoing the full therapy and in the hands of a professional therapist. In other words, it should describe what you can do and the benefits clients will receive from a visit to you. You should also include contact details such as telephone number and email address. In order to get the reader to take action you may want to offer them a discount if they use a coupon in the manual.

You can encourage local traders to take advertising space in the manual. Approach appropriate traders such as health shops, chemists and other non-competitive therapists. Using this strategy you can recover some of your production costs.

Once the mini-manual has been put together with no more than 10 to 15 pages, all your hard work is done. Reproduction does not have to be of an excessively high quality, although you might want to spend more resources on the attractiveness of the front and back pages. With the availability of desktop publishing you may decide to produce copies as and when required. If you have a large event coming up consider getting a professional printer to reproduce your mini-manual.

Some ideas for mini-manuals

- 12 Ways to Help You Stop Smoking
- 12 Ways to Help You Reduce Your Stress
- 6 Easy-to-Learn Massage Strokes
- 24 Aromatherapy Oils That Can Change Your Life

4

Education and Courses

Learning establishments of all types play a useful role for the creative therapist and may even provide the backbone for a thriving private practice.

26 PUTTING ON A FUNDRAISING EVENT

The PTAs (Parent Teacher Associations) of schools are always putting on events to raise extra income. The budget that a school receives from government or the local authority is never sufficient and events to raise extra funds can make quite a real difference to school life. The hardest part for a PTA is constantly to think of new schemes, ideas and events to encourage the parents and other members of the public to support the school.

Put yourself in the PTA's shoes and create a way of using your therapy to help boost the school's funds. For a hypnotherapist it could be to offer to run a group 'Stop Smoking' session. You could charge a fee of £20 per person and state that all monies will go to the school. Get the local media involved: radio, television, newspapers and the school newsletter.

Costs to you

- A couple of hours of your time
- Production of extra brochures

Benefits to you

- You will get free publicity for your therapy practice (try paying for that exposure in the media and you will realise what a bargain you have got!).

- The local community will love you because of your fund raising skills (also helping your reputation and image).

- Attendees and others will want to take away your therapy brochure and may contact you later for help with other issues (always carry your brochures with you).

- People may want to continue the work they started in the £20 session by coming to see you privately.

If the session is successful, people will spread the word. People talk more easily to others about a public session than if they had visited you for a more private reason.

Ideas for different therapies

- Life coach – provide a motivation seminar.

- Massage therapist – teach couples simple strokes to help each other relax.

- Reflexologist – teach a basic routine.

- Nutritionist or homeopathist – give a talk on natural remedies for ailments.

Always have plenty of brochures, take your diary with you and encourage the local media to cover the event.

 WORKING WITH SCHOOL TEACHERS

There is a myth that teachers work from 9am to 3.30 and have about 12 weeks' holiday a year. The truth is that teachers can start their day any time before 9am and finish around 5pm or much later. Then when they get home they spend their evening marking school work. They spend parts of their weekend planning lessons for the following week or catching up on administrative tasks that seem to be constantly increasing. Add to this the hassle they can get from unruly pupils, demanding parents and head teachers and governors and you may begin to understand why so many teachers reach burnout, suffer a breakdown and leave the profession.

Stress is the number one issue for teachers today. Although teachers do have set aside training days, these are mostly related to the school curriculum. Few training days if any help teachers to cope with the demands of being a teacher. You can imagine that anyone or any organisation that can help teachers to reduce their stress levels and to relax more is going to be of interest.

Approaching head teachers

This could be the opportunity for you to offer your services. You could put together a one-day training course and help teachers as a group.

1. Write to the head teachers of your local schools.
2. Detail the range of benefits your therapy offers and state what the school, teachers and pupils will gain through your therapy.
3. A week after your letter has been sent, follow it up with a telephone call.
4. Give examples of your past successes if you can.

Another idea is to arrange to visit the school on a regular basis and provide individual sessions. A practitioner who provides Indian head massage could visit the school during the lunch break and offer this service to some teachers in the staff room. Another possibility is for teachers to enjoy your therapy when they are given non-contact time (time out of the classroom).

There are many ways in which you could reach an agreement with a school to help with stress levels. You will, of course, find that head teachers, caretakers, school governors and parents will also become curious and want to use you as well. Just imagine the possibilities of word spreading beyond the school about how good your service is. This is great way to build your personal referral network.

Getting more from your course

Once you have put together a half- or one-day course and have presented it, you will have a tried and tested service which you can offer to many other establishments. All you need to do is change the emphasis from the target audience, in this case from teachers, to, for example, nurses, the police, fire crew, office workers, traffic wardens, social workers and more.

(28) WORKING WITH SCHOOL PUPILS

Children of all ages can suffer from stress and tension and there is no doubt that this impacts on their performance in the classroom. It can also affect their relationship with fellow pupils, teachers and parents.

If there was a way to help the whole school enjoy some mental and physical relaxation, then there could only be positive results. The pupils would operate from a calmer disposition and the number of disagreements and squabbles would be reduced. The mind absorbs more information when it is relaxed. Learning new material would be become easier and quicker. Retrieving that information for examinations would also be easier because recall is more efficient when the mind and body are relaxed.

For the NLP practitioner this kind of opportunity should be very easy. Visualisation coupled with the other senses is a great way of altering a person's state of mind, helping them to drift off into a reverie or daydream. The visualisation can contain some meaning or lesson (such as truth, honesty, respect for each other, etc.) which can be absorbed by the subconscious mind, adding even more to the event.

Usually, if a story of any kind is read to a class, it tends to be the last lesson of the day. If it were possible for these visualisation sessions to be held first thing in the morning, it could get the whole day off to a better start.

Not all therapies will be appropriate in this area but many can be, with a little creativity. For instance, an aromatherapist could help the children with progressive relaxation exercises. This can simply be tensing and relaxing muscle groups one by one, from the toes to the head and back again. They could advise on the best aromatherapy oils for concentration and memory enhancement.

If the pupils, no matter what age, were to start their day from a calmer place, their resources, such as memory, attitude, focus, and motivation could be greatly improved. This in turn would help the teachers with their stress levels and could really enhance school life for everyone.

29 WORKING IN COLLEGES AND UNIVERSITIES

You can take all the ideas we have looked at for schools and duplicate them for colleges, universities and any other educational establishments. However, at these places of learning you have people who are young adults and are responsible for themselves.

Recognising the needs of your target group

Some of these young adults or students will want help to cope with college life. This help might be in the usual areas of relationships, fears and lack of confidence, but many will want help with studying. If you can devise a programme to help students with studying, retaining and retrieving information and their examinations, then you will be a very popular resource.

You may opt to offer group sessions where attendees are charged a flat fee, or individual sessions with interested students. Firstly, though, you need to let the students know that you exist and what it is that you can do for them.

Approaching a college or university

Initially, try the official route through the college hierarchy. It is easier to convince them of your skills if you can boast about a previous course at another college. But, of course, you have to start somewhere. Be sure you have given prior thought to the course structure and are able to present the outline. All colleges want their students to get the highest grades, so in your initial approach emphasise how you can help with this.

Despite your good intentions and the obvious benefits, you might still get turned away. Your next strategy is to approach the Student Union. Tell them that you will provide a discounted course if they organise the venue and publicise the event. The Student Union's job is to look after their members' welfare. Hint at this aspect when you contact them. If you do get an agreement to provide a course, this will help you the following year if you decide to approach the college authorities again.

If none of the above succeeds, you can still display your notices around the college for individual sessions. Most students are short of cash so offer a reduction in fees for group sessions. For the next academic year you have gained evidence that your therapy has been used – ammunition when you approach the Student Union or college again.

Lastly, consider asking the college to provide a small room on the campus where you can offer discounted sessions to students. If you arrange to be available in this room, on a certain day and between a set time this makes it as easy as possible for the students to find you and it gives you the chance to build your reputation.

30 LIASING WITH TRAINING SCHOOLS

Anyone who takes their practice seriously will have taken a course at a recognised school and passed some form of examination. Once you have qualified there is a temptation to go out there and have little or no contact with the school. If you do this, you could be missing out on opportunities to increase your income.

Gaining referrals

Any school of good standing will get potential clients contacting them and asking for a referral to a therapist. If you maintain good relationships with your school you will obtain some of these referrals. The better the school knows you, the more confidence they will have in passing these enquiries to you.

When you are approached by someone who has been referred to you by your training school, always let the school know that you have successfully made contact with this person and that you have taken them on as a client. This assures the school that you are dealing with their enquiries in a professional manner and gives them the confidence to pass more clients your way.

Returning the favour

You can help the flow of referred clients by building a reciprocal arrangement. If you are asked to recommend a school (assuming you have been happy with your training), make sure that you not only recommend your school but that you ensure the school knows that you have done this. Get the potential student to tell the school that they heard about it through you.

When invitations arrive to mix or socialise with new students and lecturers, grab the opportunity. This is another way of keeping your name and face known at the school and keeping those referrals flowing.

(31) LECTURING

If you have ambitions towards lecturing at your training school or any other school, there are ways to help you achieve this that can also bring client referrals.

Giving your time to gain referrals

Volunteer to be an assistant on a relevant training course. You will usually only be allowed to perform this function if you have already taken and passed the course. Lecturers and tutors are always grateful for a spare pair of hands, particularly when it comes to the practical side of the course. Don't expect to get paid because you have volunteered but sometimes you may get a pleasant surprise! Remember you are getting invaluable experience at running a course for free!

Assisting on a course gives you an easy way of learning about different styles of lecturing, how a course is structured and how to manage the students. It is just one step away from running the course yourself. In an emergency the school will probably ask you to attend if the lecturer is ill or can't make it for any reason.

You can always ask the lecturer if there are any parts you can be more active in, once you have attended the course as an assistant and are feeling confident about the subject area. For example, if the module of the course is on physiology and anatomy you might want to volunteer to lecture on a part of that. This can be of great benefit to all concerned. The official lecturer gets a break but has the opportunity to intervene if they feel you have missed any important details. You get a brilliant opportunity to show your mettle as a lecturer. The students get to have someone different lecturing to them, which can help their attention and focus.

Finally, you will be perceived as an experienced therapist because you are assisting and lecturing. Students will seek your advice with their client cases. They may also pass some of the more difficult cases to you. Once more, you gain client referrals as a side effect of doing something else.

(32) SUPERVISING STUDENTS

After gaining experience in your field, you could approach your old therapy school, or any other school for that matter, and find out whether they need any new supervisors. In order to give yourself a chance of success with your approach, you must be able to prove that you have experience of being supervised. The frequency and type of supervision will vary between different schools and therapies.

Schools of good repute will have guidelines about the qualities and experience needed to become a supervisor. They should also provide a course to train you to supervise individuals and groups. Many therapy schools are now insisting that students receive supervision while they are attending a therapy course and some insist on supervision after the course is completed. For counsellors, psychotherapists and now hypnotherapists, supervision is seen as a necessity.

Adding a new dimension to your practice

Supervised sessions are paid for by the person involved. The cost to the person being supervised (student or graduate) is generally lower than for a client's therapy session, but for a supervisor it can be a useful additional income. Indeed, it can also lead to more clients. Students will come in contact with clients who have issues they feel are beyond them at their current stage of experience. The students are highly likely to pass these clients on to their supervisors. As a supervisor you can earn supervisory fees as well as gaining clients referred to you by those students.

Build up a good relationship with your student and once they graduate you may find that they still want to come to you for supervision and recommend others to do the same.

33 RUNNING EVENING CLASSES

Running a class gives you the chance to enjoy passing on your skills to others and have some security regarding your income. An evening class is usually for a set number of weeks. The financial security is gained by charging attendees in advance for the duration of the course. The class can run for six weeks, a college term, or the whole academic year. This is your choice and there are a number of ways of organising this.

Local adult education authorities are always looking for new courses to offer the community. You increase chances of your course being accepted if you are clear about areas you want to teach, can support this by emphasising the benefits attendees will gain, and have a structure of how you want to teach it.

To give you confidence, you really need to have a clear idea of what you are going to do during each class. After each session the students should leave having learnt something new and of value. If you attempt to 'pad out' your course to fill the time, this will become obvious and students will give you a poor rating when they are asked to assess the course.

If you do put together a good course and are turned down by the local authority, all is not lost. There is nothing to stop you hiring a venue and providing a private group course if you feel there is a market for it.

The advantages of the local authority are that they are responsible for all the marketing, administration and providing a room. The disadvantage is that they will stipulate the fee that you can charge per student and you will not necessarily receive all of this.

The advantages of running a private class are that you can decide what to charge and are not restricted by term times. The disadvantages are that you have to market the course and hire a venue.

Although running a course can be financially rewarding in itself, there are other ways that you can gain. Some students will want to see you for one-to-one treatment, whilst others will pass on your details to potential clients. The possibility of gaining more private work is therefore increased.

ORGANISING MONTHLY GROUPS

Once a month, organise a group of five or six people
(however many you can fit into your practice room) to
learn the basics of your therapy. Charge them some
nominal fee for attendance and make it more of an
informal occasion than a serious private session.

Training for basic skills

The idea of the group is not to train people to set up
professionally but to acquaint them with the basics so that
they could make use of their knowledge on a spouse,
partner, friend or themselves. This will not take business
away from you because you are merely showing them what
they can achieve with a little knowledge. If the person they
practise on enjoys the basics of the therapy they may well
come to see you to get the full professional treatment.

Make your practice brochures available, as members of
the group may want to see you privately. Ensure they all
go away with your business card because they will talk
about what they learnt to work colleagues, family and
friends and it provides another opportunity to gain
referrals.

The group meeting should be no longer than three hours
and an evening is generally the most popular time. Having
the meeting once a month gives you plenty of time to
prepare but also doesn't interfere with your private
practice.

Ideas for groups

- Aromatherapist – give talks about different oils and
  their therapeutic qualities.

- NLP therapist – help the group recognise old outdated
  patterns. Show ways of replacing them with effective
  life strategies.

- Shiatsu practitioner – talk about the theory. Show some
  simple techniques.

As the therapist you get paid for your time and expertise and you increase the possibility of more client referrals. If the evenings become very popular you may need to look for a bigger venue but the increase in attendance fees should cover any expense.

35 OFFERING CORPORATE WORKSHOPS

There are in existence thousands of companies of different sizes and shapes. With the exception of sole traders they all have one thing in common: they employ people. They need people in order to be successful and so you might say that people are their number one asset.

People are complex beings and have differing needs and wants. The importance of people to companies has become more evident and is reflected in the Personnel Department now being called the Human Resources Department. More companies are recognising that a happy and contented workforce can mean more efficient and effective employees which will then feed through positively into the bottom line – profits.

Helping to maintain a happy workforce

Companies are more open to ways of helping to keep their workforce happy and at their peak performance for as long as possible. They have recognised that it takes more than paying a weekly or monthly wage to do this. If you can recognise the needs of the company and its personnel, and offer a way of helping to fulfil those needs, then you increase your chances of securing corporate work.

Before your first approach, you must step into your customer's shoes and see matters from their perspective. What can you do for them? They want to know what benefit they will get from using your services. Once you have recognised the benefits you can provide you are ready to contact them.

Approaching companies

Companies vary tremendously in the number of employees they have and the profitability of the business, as well as their culture. What will appeal to one company will be rejected outright by another. Your initial approach must be to find out the name of the person who has the power to say yes or no to your service. Telephone the company and ask the operator for the name of someone in the Human Resources Department. Have a chat with the person concerned. The idea of this call is not, I repeat not, to find out if they are interested in your therapy. It is to find out who makes the decisions about workshops and courses for the company. You want the person's name and title. When you have this information you end the conversation by saying you will write to them.

Be clear on what you are offering the company. Don't be vague or give too much choice. Write a letter to the name you have acquired and follow the AIDA principle mentioned in Chapter 6 on 'Newspapers'. Enclose a brochure giving more details about the course you are offering and stating the price. This will save you having to put too much detail in the covering letter. Try to let them know that you are knowledgeable about their industry. The more they feel you understand them, the more likely they are to look at your service favourably.

When you send the letter, make a note in your diary to follow this up with a telephone call no longer than a week later. Following the letter with a telephone call shows that you mean business. If your contact says that they haven't had time to read it, tell them you will ring back the next day. If they have passed it on to someone else to deal with, find out that person's name and speak to them immediately. If you get a rejection, find out why. This will help you improve your approach to the next company.

Do not undersell yourself. Generally you can charge double and sometimes triple your normal private rate. Appearing cheap will not help their perception of the quality of your service. Training companies often charge per person or will state a price for up to five people and then 10 people, and so on.

Corporate work can be very rewarding financially. It may even take you away from individual private practice to providing purely group work.

(36) WORKING WITH LOCAL COUNCILS

Just as there is scope to secure business from private clients and corporate clients so you should not overlook your local councils. Although every household and business comes under the jurisdiction of a particular council, you do not have to restrict yourself because of this. Contact the councils in the surrounding area that are within a reasonable travelling distance for you.

Councils have many departments to handle cleansing, rates, legal matters, recreation, traffic, political matters and education, to name a few. All these departments employ many people who could benefit from your therapy. Just like corporations, you need to let councils know that you exist and what you can offer their employees. You can approach the Human Resources division and follow a similar marketing plan to that described under 'Offering Corporate Workshops' in this chapter.

Keeping your finger on the pulse

Receiving a regular copy of the council's newsletter can be a very useful source of information. From this publication and any others, you will find out useful contact names within the council but also find out on what particular social matter the council is focussing. If you feel you are able to offer them a workshop to help with their latest initiative, then approach them. They will be more open to a service that supports their own schemes than if you were trying to start up some completely new initiative of your own.

If you manage to support a council initiative and secure a role for your therapy, many wonderful benefits can come your way. You may find that as the council promotes its own chosen causes, whether for internal (council employees) or external (the public) consumption, your name and therapy is included in the promotion. This gives you a higher profile in your local community. As a result you can find that you get a sudden influx of new private clients. Local newspapers are always looking for information on unusual activities in the area and you may just find yourself the subject of an article under a headline such as:

Council Uses Reiki to Heal Tensions

5

Directories

You must have your contact details in places where potential customers would expect to find you.

(37) THE *YELLOW PAGES*

For so long now, this publication has been the main source of finding anyone in any trade. How long this directory will remain the number one choice is anyone's guess, but with the advent of the internet and on-line directories it seems logical to conclude that its days may be numbered. However, that may still be somewhat in the future. The point is to remind you to think about how much return you are getting from your advertising budget and not to renew past contracts merely out of habit.

At the moment, taking an entry in the *Yellow Pages* is, with a few exceptions, a winner. Many people assume that any company or organisation that appears in the *Yellow Pages* must be an established business and reasonably long term. The 'cowboys' tend to put a splash of adverts in a local newspaper today and are gone tomorrow. There is a kind of respectability that your business can enjoy from appearing in the *Yellow Pages*.

Designing your advertisement

When it comes to designing your advert, as with all mediums, serious thought and consideration are needed. Although size isn't everything, it seems to make a difference here. The more impact you can achieve, the more clients will notice you and telephone your practice. Impact can be bought by having a bigger advert than your rivals. However many advertisers spoil their entry by cramming too much detail into it. A customer scanning the *Yellow Pages* will rarely bother with a crammed advert because it is not easy on the eye. Plenty of white space, or in this case yellow space, makes the text stand out and attracts the reader.

Look through different editions of the *Yellow Pages* and particularly at the entries of your competitors. With your type of therapy or service there may be an accepted style. Go through the process of pretending to be a potential client. Based on the existing adverts decide which therapist you would go to and why their advert attracts you. This will give you the basis for your own design.

A medium sized advert, with plenty of space, that has an emotional appeal and clearly states the essential details, will beat a larger and 'messy' advert every time. As humans we tend to make decisions based on emotions and then afterwards arrive at a logical reason to support that decision. Aim for the emotions, but also include logic in the smaller details.

(38) OTHER DIRECTORIES

There are many other directories published by different bodies and companies. Whilst it is always a good idea to aim to let people know you exist in as many places as possible, there are some common factors that can persuade you for or against inclusion.

Estimating success from other directories

The number one factor is return on investment. You need to estimate the likelihood of anyone finding you in these directories. Compare like with like and contrast the cost and popularity. For example, there are other telephone directories that duplicate the service provided by the *Yellow Pages*. The *Thomson Local* directory is in this category but has the added advantage that the directory is delivered to every household. The *Yellow Pages* is delivered to households with telephones only. The rates for advertising are less than in the *Yellow Pages* but, according to popular opinion, the majority of potential customers who have telephones turn to the *Yellow Pages* first.

Other directories can be national or local. They may accept listings from certain businesses only. There are a number of complementary or alternative therapy directories in existence. The longer you are in business the more sales calls you will receive from these organisations trying to convince you that it is essential for the success of your business to be listed in their directory. Be careful here. It is so easy to get caught up in the hype and throw your advertising budget away.

Before committing yourself

1. Look at a copy of the directory.
2. Find out how, where and when the directory is distributed.
3. If certain establishments (libraries, clinics, etc.) are sent copies, check this out.
4. Telephone past advertisers and find out how successful their advert has been.

Some directories are produced by therapy associations. An entry in this directory is sometimes included in the annual membership fee or there may be a separate charge. It is well worth having an entry in your own association's directory, even if it is just a few lines.

(39) TALKING PAGES

This service is currently run by *Yellow Pages* but there are other organisations such as Scoot that offer a similar service. Basically, a potential customer telephones Talking Pages and tells the operator the type of service they want to contact (Psychic, Colour Practitioner, etc.) and the location they want. The operator will then give the caller one business's telephone number and up to three others.

The choice given to the customer depends on the number of businesses that are listed.

If you are the only business listed under your category, you will get all the customers that use this facility. If there are two businesses then your business will rotate between first and second place. It also means you are likely to receive half the business available through this medium. Even so, that might be more than adequate to be profitable.

Before committing yourself
1. Ask the company to provide statistics of the number of callers wanting your type of service in your location.
2. Pretend to be a customer and try the service.
3. Telephone the competition and see what they think of the service.

You cannot assume that just because a telephone number is accepted by the customer, they will actually call you. With this in mind, an additional service (with an additional cost) is now being offered where the caller is put directly through to your telephone. The idea is to grab the customer while they are keen and to cut down on the possibility of their having second thoughts.

6

Advertising Plus!

With adequate research and analysis, advertising can be profitable in the short and long term.

40 NEWSPAPERS

The thought may come to you as you read your daily newspaper and notice adverts for loans, courses and other products and services, that you could also promote yourself here. This isn't necessarily as silly as it may sound. It does depend on what you want to promote.

If your business consists of a practice in one location only, forget about advertising nationally. Your clients will not travel much beyond 10 or 15 miles to see you unless you have a national reputation or offer something that is a rarity or speciality. Realistically you should only expect to attract people from your locality, in which case you may as well stick to your local newspaper and get better coverage for your money.

Alternatively, if you have a number of practices around the country, if you are undertaking a national lecture tour or if you are selling a product via mail order, then national newspaper advertising could well be worth a longer look.

Tips for researching national advertising
1. Read and make notes (which detail the following points) from all the daily newspapers over the period of a week at least.
2. Who are the type of people who read each newspaper? Publications are available from any library's reference section that give these details. Generally, you will want

to aim at people who have a reasonable disposable income.
3. When are the best days and which are the best sections to promote your therapy?
4. Is the newspaper running features or articles that could support your marketing?
5. Get your advert positioned close to any relevant articles.
6. Do not accept the first piece of space offered you.
7. Will a one off or a series of adverts be beneficial?
    - Look at other advertisers and see what they do.
    - Compare like with like.
    - Ask the newspaper advertising staff for their opinion.

Before designing your advertisement think about your target audience. Who is your client? If you aim at everyone your advert will not have any focus. Aim at the type of person or problem you want to help. Once you have decided who you are aiming at, there are a number of principles involved with advert design that are applicable to other promotional aids such as posters, flyers and leaflets.

AIDA principles
'AIDA' stands for Attraction (or Attention), Interest, Desire, Action. Bear these principles in mind and your advert will be as effective as possible.

Attraction or Attention
You will have a very short space of time to attract your audience. If you don't get their attention, no matter how good the rest of your advert is, you will have lost your reader. Some of the better words to gain someone's attention are FREE or NEW or UNIQUE. Be brief with your attention grabber. Try to use less than five words. Never use the words 'I' or 'We' but use the word 'You' instead. Often an advert will ask a question and the idea is to get 'yes' answers. For example 'Are you stressed out?' If the reader responds with a mental 'yes', they will feel that this advert is aimed at them and will read on.

Interest

Okay, you now have their attention and need to hold onto it. Readers get bored very quickly, so don't blind them with science. Think the way your reader thinks and put yourself in their position. Do not flog your cranio-sacral therapy at this point. Sell the 'sizzle' not the 'sausage'. Tell them that you can relieve headaches and migraines and release tension in their muscles.

Desire

In the 'interest' aspect you may have used negatives. In the 'desire' aspect, switch to positives such as 'feel calmer and more in control' or 'relax and take things in your stride'. In other words, you tap into the 'desire' of the reader to improve their life.

Action

This is where you encourage your reader to take action. Make it as easy as possible for them. At times people need to be told what to do next. Use action statements: 'To relax today telephone 0800 EASY LIFE now'. Highlight a 'use by' date if you are making a special offer. This way people are more likely to take action now rather than miss out on the special deal. You could use the phrase, '20% discount to the first 20 callers on 0800 EASY LIFE'.

Thoughts for successful advert design

1. **Focus on your clients.**
   - Why would they come to you?
   - What will they gain?

2. **Highlight benefits more than features.**
   - You might be skilled in the latest techniques and have the most modern equipment but what will your client get from it?

3. **Work at your headline.**
   - Write a minimum of 20 headlines before deciding which one is best.
   - Include the most attractive words such as; Free, New, Amazing, Now, Announcing, How To, At Last, Here, Today.

4. **Use a relaxed style.**
   - Write using informal and/or local phrases.
   - Use short, punchy sentences.

5. **Drop the technicalities.**
   - Don't confuse the reader with jargon or mnemonics (unless you are using it to raise their curiosity).

6. **Don't write *War and Peace.***
   - Don't waffle or use 20 words when six will do.
   - Keep details focussed.

7. **Give instructions.**
   - Tell them what to do: 'Phone Now' or 'Send the Completed Form Today'.

8. **Check it.**
   - Get someone to edit your advert for grammar and spelling.
   - Make sure obvious essential details are included (telephone number, address, etc.).

Other design tips

- Make your advert easy to read by making sensible use of bold, italic and differing sizes of typeface, but don't overdo it.

- Use a mix of upper and lower case letters for headlines to make them easier to read.

- The minor details at the bottom of the advert should include your name.

- Include some designations but no more than four.

- Incorporate words like 'professional', 'qualified', 'experienced' when referring to yourself.

Local newspapers

Here rates should be much lower and enable you to afford an advert that provides better exposure. But size isn't everything. You don't have to always use a display type advertisement. Sometimes the regular classified type of advertisement can be effective if you opt for a series over a number of weeks. Take a look at your rival's adverts and decide which of them works the best and why. Given the choice, which one would you want to telephone for an appointment? When you know why, then you are ready to design your own classified advertisement, but don't imitate, think how can you improve on your competition.

When you are ready to approach the newspaper to take advertising space, always ask for discounts. If you don't ask you won't get! In particular, when you want to place a display type advertisement enquire about the newspaper's policy on last minute space. This is when the deadline for printing is almost due but there is still space to be filled. Often the newspaper will give away the space at a much reduced rate in order to fill it. Sometimes you can be offered a whole page for the price that you would normally pay for a tenth of that size.

Whatever publication you decide to advertise in, always drive a hard bargain and make the most of your marketing budget.

(41) MAGAZINES

Thousands of magazines are produced in this country that focus on hundreds of subjects. There are also magazines imported from other countries. But just like with advertising in a national newspaper, if you are not careful you could easily be throwing your money away and learning a very expensive lesson.

Should I advertise in a national magazine?

Only if you can offer a product or service nationally should you consider advertising in a national magazine. The only exceptions to this rule are if your returns from local customers who find you through this medium are sufficient to cover your outlay or your service is so specialised that people will be willing to travel the length or breadth of the country. You might be pleasantly surprised how far someone is willing to travel to see you as you become better known.

Choosing which magazines to advertise with is the next dilemma. For an aromatherapist who specialises in helping people with arthritis, it maybe more obvious. An advert in *Arthritis Today* or any of the other publications on this subject may prove to be rewarding. On the other hand, a stress counsellor may want to advertise in *The Teacher* which is a quarterly magazine. An osteopath may find advertising in a football magazine profitable.

To be successful, you must think about the type of person that reads the magazine and their lifestyle. From a profile of the reader, you should be able to conclude what service appeals to them. A beauty therapist may not have as much return through advertising in a football magazine (although more women are attending football matches so it may well be a new and untapped opportunity). Time changes everything. Never restrict yourself with outdated stereotypes of the population. On the other hand, revolution can take time, focus on certainties and take chances only once you are established and can afford to do so.

(42) NEWSLETTERS

Here is a relatively inexpensive but focused way of getting your practice known. Newsletters exist in the thousands. With the advent of the computer and desktop printer, the production costs of newsletters have become so affordable that even the smallest group, organisation or society can put together a very respectable looking publication. Newsletters vary in size, content and subject. Often the membership fees pay for the production of the newsletter and any income though advertising is a bonus to the organisation.

Although there are countless newsletters produced, obtaining a copy can be more difficult. If the organisation is private and has a closed membership you may never acquire a copy, unless you are a member or know someone who is a member. Alternatively, some organisations will supply copies of their current edition to local libraries. You should then be able to gain an idea of the content and whether placing an advert will be worthwhile.

Many people will keep every copy of a newsletter that they receive, particularly when the articles are interesting. So, although when you first advertise you may not get the response you hoped for, you could be pleasantly surprised at how many enquires you receive long afterwards.

Rates can vary tremendously, but because costs are lower and circulation is not large a display type advert should be quite affordable. You will probably be able to secure a decent sized space and possibly be able to place it on the front or back of the newsletter for added exposure.

You can assist your marketing effort and gain more exposure if you can write an article that discusses your therapy and its relevance to the aims of the newsletter's organisation. You can negotiate with the editor for the amount of space you would like and may even want to make it a condition of advertising. The experienced negotiator may persuade the editor to give space for an article without having to purchase advertising space. Just like with newspapers, editors of newsletters find it difficult to find enough articles to fill the pages. You can use this to your advantage and save your marketing budget for something else.

43 RADIO

Here is a medium that is often overlooked. Marketing via your local radio station can be more affordable than you think. The obvious approach is to consider advertising with the station. Some stations supply the whole package for you including a jingle and assistance with the best way to communicate your message. You also have the option of designing the commercial yourself.

Researching local stations

1. What choice of local radio stations do I have?
2. Which station attracts the biggest audience?
3. What type of audience does the station attract? (e.g. pensioners, mothers, teenagers, etc.) and at which time of the day?
4. What type of audience do I want my advertisement aimed at?
5. Do I want to use my voice or someone else's?
6. Should I include music and/or other sounds?
7. What is the message I am trying to get across?
8. What is the essential information I must mention? (contact details, location)

Spend some time listening to the local radio stations and the adverts in particular. This will give you ideas about the type of advertising that would best suit your service and how to present it in a professional way. The radio station should also be able to provide guidance to help you make the most of your air-time.

Gaining free exposure

Again, there is a way of gaining exposure without parting with any of your hard-earned money. Radio stations are always on the look-out for an interesting story or event. Simply use the same tactics that you used with your local newspaper and also refer to the sections on Articles and/or Competitions in this chapter. If you get involved with any charity event or with a school fundraiser, let the radio station know what you are doing. Inform them as soon as you can before it happens so that you and your practice gain the maximum exposure.

Another way of using the radio is to offer the station an informational programme. You could volunteer to be interviewed about your therapy, your practice and the issues you help with. If you are lucky, you might persuade some past clients to talk about how your therapy has helped them. Nothing promotes the benefits of your therapy more than first-hand accounts of real people's experiences. You might even encourage the station to produce a series of programmes about different complementary therapies. The result: you get free advertising and the radio station gets an interesting programme for its listeners. If you are good, you may even be able to turn it into a regular feature.

(44) TELEVISION

There are so many television channels broadcasting now that the opportunities to be on local or national TV are much easier. At times you may even be approached by a television company to appear on a particular programme.

Paid for advertising is still very expensive and so the best way to market yourself on television is to be a guest on an appropriate programme. Think of all the chat shows there are now, morning, afternoon, evening and late night shows. These shows might feature a certain type of therapy or be about a particular ailment. Often the subject of future programmes will be announced several weeks in advance. If you feel the subject is relevant to your therapy, contact the programme makers. If you can convince the makers that you can help with the subject area, you will not find it difficult to secure an invitation to join the programme.

Recently there has been a tendency to put together documentary programmes on the effectiveness of certain therapies in dealing with a particular problem. For example, the efficacy of hypnotherapy, NLP, cognitive therapy, counselling and others can be tested on people who have phobias. This is fine, as long as you get a result. Be aware that programme makers are only interested in a quick result and will have an effect on the therapy, just by being present. You really need to give careful consideration before allowing cameras into your therapy room. For those who do take this step the rewards can be an instant reputation and clients wanting to see you from all over the country. Generally, the client will be provided by the TV company and will be well aware of what is involved with regard to the lack of confidentiality. As the therapist you may also want to add your reassurance about how you will handle exceptional circumstances if they arise.

> One therapist known to me appeared on a television programme about phobias and received over 200 calls from people who wanted her help with their phobia.

(45) BILLBOARD ADVERTISING

Forget about the gigantic billboards that you see on the side of buildings or motorways as these would be highly unlikely to generate anything like the amount of business you would need to make them economically viable. The billboards that can be successful are those at your local bus station or railway station. If you live in the city you might consider the underground or other public transport system for advertising.

Paying for billboards at stations that are not close to your practice location would be wasteful. Negotiate with the company responsible to rent the billboard at your local station. One of the best locations is the platforms at the station. Commuters and other travellers need something to do whilst waiting for the next train to arrive. This is your opportunity to capture their attention with a well-designed and well-placed advertisement.

The advertisement should let them know the benefits of

treatment, the type of treatment you offer, ailments you help, a contact number and that you are a local business. In fact, you should cover a similar amount of detail to any of your other display advertisements. Do not overcrowd the space you have with too many details. Study other companies' designs and decide what you feel works and what doesn't to give you a better idea. Another option is to employ an expert to do this for you.

Other billboard locations

- Sheltered bus stops

- Local shopping centres

- Local airports

- Taxis and some mini cabs

- Buses – on the inside and outside

(46) LOCAL AUTHORITY PUBLICATIONS

Your local borough council or authority will have their own publications for communicating their goals and objectives to the local community. They will want to be seen to be supporting local business because of the wider benefits this positive approach can bring in terms of direct revenue, jobs and custom for other businesses.

The editors of these publications will be interested in any article of an unusual nature. They can be quite supportive of your need for publicity, and give you space to promote yourself. The good news is that this is free publicity! It also gets you known to other businesses and may lead to some corporate work, where your fees can be on the higher side.

An added bonus is if your local council produces a glossy magazine of activities, events and news in the area. Copies of these magazines are provided to numerous local organisations and to public access facilities such as libraries and community projects. From this not only will local businesses become aware of your services but also the general public.

With this type of free publicity you can enjoy a perception of quality about your services. People will generally have the impression that your appearance in the council magazine means you must be professional, trustworthy and meet the highest standards.

Your approach to the editor of the magazine should be to request free editorial – use the angle that you are letting them know about a new local service to the community. If your service is unique then you will have little problem in gaining that space. If you are offering something that is in abundance in your locality you will need to think of some feature that makes what you offer different from the competition. You may find that offering some discount or a free initial trial is enough to get you coverage.

47 CONTINUITY OR BREAKS

Many marketing experts support the view that continuity is an essential part of any successful campaign. Instead of advertising for one week in a local newspaper, you are likely to get a better response if you continue to advertise for a series of weeks.

This takes into account the cummulative effect of your advert. If a potential client sees your advert on the first week they may well not follow it through, although a seed will have been planted. If they then see it a second week, that seed may have grown sufficiently to convince them to telephone. For other potential clients it may take three, four weeks or more.

From this you may conclude that to have a regular weekly presence must be the best approach. Logic seems to support this view, as some readers do not buy the newspaper every week and others will not see the advert in the first few weeks. Certainly some therapists confirm that booking space for the year not only works very well for them but also gives them the added advantage of being able to negotiate a large discount.

On the other hand, breaks in your advertising can also help convince potential clients that they need to take action. Some readers will have seen your advert in the newspaper every week. They may feel that they could benefit from your service but because they see your advert every week, they don't feel the need to do it now. If you stopped advertising for a few weeks, there would be some people who would then be annoyed that they hadn't written down your number or cut the advert out. They would come to the decision that if they ever saw your advert again, they would definitely follow it through. A few weeks later when your advert reappears, the break encourages them to take immediate action.

So both strategies can work quite successfully for you. The added advantage of booking smaller blocks of advertising space, say five weeks, is that the initial outlay is not so great and you get a chance to change newspapers if the response is poor.

48 WRITING ARTICLES

How would you like to promote your business for free in a way that gets you the kind of impact that would usually cost you hundreds if not thousands of pounds. Newspapers, particularly local newspapers, find it difficult to fill all the space they have available. They are always looking for local stories that are of interest to their readership.

This is where you can help them and yourself. Write an article which promotes your business. The article must be topical and unusual to be accepted. Despite all that available space, the editor won't publish just anything.

If you buy the local paper regularly you will get a flavour of the type of story they like. You can include a charity connection about helping the local community. Once you get into the right frame of mind, many, many ideas can be formulated. For instance, a headline could be:

88

Local Indian Head Masseur Helps Fire Brigade Relax Between Calls

Another could be:

Stop Smoking Evening Raises Funds for Local School

Ideas to help you
Ask yourself:

Q. What are the benefits of my therapy?

A. E.g. stress reduction, memory enhancement, confidence boosting.

Q. What groups of people could benefit from these?

A. Stress reduction – emergency services
Memory enhancement – students
Confidence boosting – job seekers

Q. Who do I need to approach to set this up?

A. Local Fire Brigade
Police station
Schools, colleges
Employment office

Managing the session
1. Offer your time free to these organisations, but set limits.
2. If possible try to do a group session.
3. If you can't do group sessions give 15-minute taster sessions.
4. Ensure the group you help understands that part of the arrangement is to allow the local newspaper to run a feature on the session.
5. Give the newspaper at least one week's notice; more if possible. Be aware of their deadlines.
6. Get your practice name, address and telephone number incorporated into the article.

7. Include other ailments and problems that your therapy can help.
8. Take a supply of your brochures and business cards with you.
9. Carry your appointments diary with you.

(49) RUNNING COMPETITIONS

People love to enter competitions. Look through any magazine or newspaper, national or local, and you will find a number of them. The prizes can range from a holiday for two in Mauritius to a £20 discount voucher at Marks and Spencer.

Here is your chance to gain some free publicity at the expense of providing a prize. The exposure should more than compensate for any cost you incur. In reality it is easier to place your competition in a local newspaper. They will love the idea because you are filling their space and are giving something to the readers.

You usually get the chance to write your own article with a competition. This gives you a great and cost-effective way of publicising your practice. Do not go mad and give away too much. Even if you only give away four sessions of treatment, by the time the last person, (number 4) has arrived, you will start to begrudge the free treatment you are giving. It would be better to give no more than two treatments and if possible, only one.

The usual wording is something like:

The Stanthorpe Times has teamed up with the Freedom Therapy Practice to offer you the chance to win a free Aromatherapy massage.

Go on to mention the different types of treatment you offer and their benefits. In addition, consider including a discount coupon for those who book a session by a certain date. Include a 'use by' date on the coupon.

In a feature this might be written as:

'And that's not all! The *Stanthorpe Times* has negotiated a special £5 discount off any treatment offered at the Freedom Therapy Practice for our readers. So everyone can be a winner now!'

Include a contact telephone number and possibly the address of the practice. You may receive clients who don't use the coupon but book a session and pay the full amount. Either way, you are getting your practice known and this type of exposure would ordinarily cost you several times what you lose on the free session and discount coupons.

7

Organisations, Groups and Societies

Joining forces with established bodies can give you access to many new markets for very little expense.

(50) NATIONAL DAYS

As well as official national holidays like Christmas, New Year, Easter and bank holidays, there are a whole host of other days, even weeks, to promote different messages.

Examples of national awareness campaigns

- National Stop Smoking Day
- Heart Disease Awareness Day
- Cancer Awareness Week
- Stress Awareness Day
- Save the Children Week
- National Phobia Week

Many organisations have adopted a date during the year when they get a chance to focus the public's attention on their issue. National and local newspapers, television and radio will usually give editorial space to these dates to raise awareness.

If you have advance warning of these particular days they can be a great opportunity for your practice. If you can offer a treatment to assist with an ailment or issue relevant to the national day, then you are likely to gain free publicity for yourself. Just approach your friendly newspaper editor and offer them an article that has a direct connection to the day and what you can do to help. You may get a feature without having to do anything else. However, you are more likely to succeed if you offer some form of free treatment or trial.

Connecting your therapy to national campaigns

- Polarity therapist – arrange a free energy balancing session for local nurses.

- Acupuncturist – offer 10-minute sessions to people with phobias.

- Nutritionist – provide a mini workshop for people with high cholesterol levels.

- Colour healer – manage a group session for cancer sufferers at the local hospice.

Look at the benefits your therapy offers and match those benefits with the issue that the national date is highlighting.

51 AILMENT ORGANISATIONS AND GROUPS

There are numerous organisations that offer help to individuals who suffer from a particular ailment. When conventional medicine is unable to provide successful treatment, people naturally look to other means. Some motivated individuals start to put together a data bank of useful tips and tried and trusted remedies and then make this information available to others. From these humble beginnings many essential societies and support groups have started and they often go on to gain national status.

Within these organisations are people who are open to alternative treatments. They may even be more aware how your therapy can help their particular ailment than you. You can make contact with the national body if one exists or contact the local support group directly. A quick trip to your local library will arm you with a large number of these groups' details.

Examples of local and national groups

- Phobics Anonymous
- Victim Support
- Arthritis Care
- ME Support Groups
- Breathe Easy Asthma Groups
- MS Support

Approaching groups

1. Telephone the group organiser and introduce yourself.
   – talk about the ailment using appropriate language.
   – mention past successful cases if you can.
   – describe the benefits your therapy provides.
   (This approach tends to be more successful than writing a formal letter and allows you to build good relationship with the organiser.)
2. Volunteer your services for free initially until some trust is built up and results are seen.
3. After a trial period, ask for minimum donations to cover your time and costs.

As a volunteer therapist you may want to start your initial therapy with a group session. If, however, you can only deal with individuals, you could organise 10- or 15-minute sessions for those who are not familiar with your therapy.

Through this marketing method you can gain a reputation for helping people with a particular ailment and can legitimately say you specialise in this area. It also looks good on your CV if you apply for a paid position at a clinic. You can gain greater exposure through the support group's internal communications, such as their newsletters. Local newspapers and national dailies may be interested in running an article on 'Reflexology and How it Helps MS

Sufferers' or 'How Aromatherapy Eases Asthma Symptoms', for example.

From the expertise you gain in this area, you can organise workshops to train other therapists with the methods you have found to be most successful. Members of the groups may also want to secure your services at your private practice and will be willing to pay your normal rate.

52 SUPPORTING A CHARITY

Wouldn't it be great if you were able to raise funds for your favourite local charity and add another dimension to your marketing? It would seem like one of those wonderful but rare situations where everybody wins. Yet it is quite possible to organise this.

Managing the arrangement

1. Write in the first instance to your chosen charity.
   – Offer to provide therapy for a special 'one off' event.
   – Agree a nominal client fee (e.g. £10) which will go to the charity.
   – use the AIDA principles described in Chapter 6, under 'Newspapers', to persuade the charity that your event would be a success.
2. Follow up your letter with a phone call a week later if necessary.
3. Make use of the charity's organisational ability and get them
   – to take responsibility for securing a venue
   – to set up the facilities such as a stand or room (local sports centres or shopping centres have plenty of passing trade).
4. Ensure that the charity informs all the local newspapers, radio and television stations about the event.

At face value it seems that you are giving away your time and expertise for no return. However, you will get much more back. You get free publicity for you, your therapy and your practice through the press coverage. It is vitally important to get your practice details and the ailments you can help with mentioned in the newspaper article. Every person who takes up the offer of a £10 session gives you a captive audience. Give them one of your practice leaflets and tell them how much more you can accomplish in a full session. Talk about some anonymous case histories.

Getting more from the event

1. Offer a discount on any session that is booked on the day of the event.
2. Have your diary with you, as some people will want to book straight away and you want to capture them while they are still receptive to the idea.
3. Arrange a noticeboard showing the ailments and conditions you can help with. This makes it easier for passing trade to find out more about you.
4. Have the name of your practice and a contact telephone number clearly visible.
5. Persuade someone to hand out your practice brochures to everyone passing. Make sure you have plenty of these printed, as you will need them.

Once you have decided to make this offer, your commitment must be 100%. Throw every marketing tool you can into the ring and convince everyone that they will feel better for having your therapy.

(53) SPEAKING TO SOCIAL GROUPS

Social meetings and gatherings, including men's and women's clubs, are always looking for new and interesting speakers. It can be an endless nightmare for the organisers of such groups to continually have to come up with new ideas, speakers and places to visit. The members want to be entertained and enjoy their membership. Here is another win-win situation where you satisfy their requirement for a guest speaker and you find more clients.

Go to your local library and find out the names and addresses of all the social groups within a reasonable travelling distance. Then telephone one of the organisers, have an informal chat or write to them telling them what you do. Tell them you are available as a guest speaker and are willing to come along and give free demonstrations or provide a group session.

Managing your speaking engagement

1. Have your speech prepared.
2. Know your subject inside out.
3. Consider any equipment you will need.
4. Be punctual and stick to your allotted time.
5. Keep it light and fun if possible. Don't get bogged down in technical jargon.
6. Have a few anecdotes ready to tell.
7. If you can, include some practical demonstrations.
8. Always ask for questions at the end of your speech. It gets people to think about how they would like to be helped by your therapy.
9. Have plenty of brochures with you.

At the end of your talk don't be in too much of a hurry to leave. There will always be people who will want to have a private word with you about their issue. Bring your diary with you so that you can take bookings.

Typical groups to approach

- Women's Institute
- Townswomen's Guild
- Lions Clubs
- Rotary Clubs
- Rotaract Clubs
- Amateur Dramatic Societies

- Over 50s/60s clubs

- Pensioner's social groups

- Hospital League of Friends

54 BENEFITTING FROM RELIGIOUS CONNECTIONS

If you are of a particular faith why not let those in your community know about your skills? Most religious groups will want ways of finding extra funding for numerous projects. If you can help them in any way you will get their co-operation, which in turn can help you to attract more clients.

Given permission, you could make use of a noticeboard in your place of worship. You increase your chances of getting agreement if you donate part of your fees to the organisation. Many religious organisations organise a fete or fair to raise funds for certain causes. Use your skills to help these causes by providing taster sessions and donating your fees during these events and you increase your standing in the community. This can gain you free local publicity.

Another way to attract clients through your place of worship is to offer discounts to fellow members. Don't expect to be inundated with clients but you do increase the possibilities of gaining more business by doing this.

Within any national or local religious group, there will always be smaller organisations that take responsibility for different matters. You will find newspapers being produced weekly or monthly, as well as many newsletters. There may be a restoration fund committee and a special appeals committee and many others all trying to raise funds.

Generally it helps if you belong to the group and are a regular worshipper, but don't let this stop you from approaching any religious group with an offer.

DOING VOLUNTEER WORK

A way of cutting your teeth and gaining experience in a particular area of the community is volunteer work. During your slackest day for private clients, offer your services to a local organisation. This can be a support group for the homeless or a drop-in centre for people who are HIV positive or indeed any organisation whose cause you would like to support.

Approach the organisation as a volunteer therapist. This is the way many new therapists develop their skills quickly in their field and gain experience of a particular issue. As they progress the issue might even become their area of expertise. Although you should not expect to be paid, some organisations will pay you a nominal fee or cover your travelling expenses.

The organisation should provide the room that you will use and because you are a resident therapist, will normally allow you to place your leaflets and posters about their building. You will also find that you are mentioned in articles in their newsletter.

The organisation might even want to inform the local media that they can now offer your kind of therapy. This encourages more users to attend and other therapists to volunteer their services. You gain free publicity and get the opportunity to network with the other therapists. This helps reduce the isolation often felt by therapists. Effective organisations will invite you to attend an induction course to acquaint you with their procedures and give you more background about their particular issue.

With this association the organisation acquires another therapy for their client group. Your knowledge of the client group and how your service can help a particular ailment expands. In addition, you may also expect a glowing reference in the future should you need one!

DEALING WITH TELESALES CALLERS

If you have taken out advertising in the *Yellow Pages*, companies will telephone you and attempt to sell you their services. Many of these telesales calls will be from companies wanting to sell client-generating promotion schemes. Be careful or you could find yourself with an increase in expenses but little in the way of new clients.

The telesales staff have been trained with a particular sales patter to convince you of all the benefits of their scheme. They will make it seem almost impossible not to be successful and imply that if you don't grab this opportunity first, your rival will. Don't be fooled! If it is that good, they will still be around next year.

Some companies play on your generosity or your guilt. They will be working on behalf of a charity and want you to take out an advert in a calendar or information brochure, for example. They won't directly ask for money, but very craftily ask for your support. They will use words like, 'will you support the poor people in your community?' It is very difficult to say no, but if you want to stop yourself becoming poor as well and losing your business, you must! Tell them that you have your own charities that you support and that your marketing budget has been used. Only take them up on their offer if you do genuinely want to support some disadvantaged group this way. Just don't expect this to achieve any worthwhile response.

Remember, you do not have to say yes to every advertising opportunity, even though you may be pressured into meeting some artificial deadline. Insist on seeing the product you may be advertising in and always negotiate a better rate than the one you are initially quoted.

WORKING WITH DRIVING SCHOOLS

Look through your local directory and you will find many driving schools listed. Some schools are national organisations and others are just a 'one man band'. Whatever size of school, they all occasionally have pupils whose nerves get the better of them. Their driving ability might be perfectly acceptable but on the day of the test their nervousness means that they make mistakes and fail.

The driving instructor has done all that they can as far as passing on the skills which are required to drive the car. What they often are unable to do is help those students who have a problem with their nerves and lack confidence. Such students provide opportunities for you.

Some therapies such as hypnotherapy and NLP are more adept at helping in this area, but virtually all types of therapy offer directly or indirectly a form of relaxation. If you couple your therapy with some visualisation exercises you will help any client to reduce their nerves and feel calmer. There is no doubt that when we feel calm, we feel more in control of ourselves and confident.

Write to driving schools and tell them that you offer a programme to help nervous student drivers. Enclose a couple of business cards. If you can, show quotes from past clients as testimonials to the effectiveness of your therapy skills. Not only do you give yourself the chance of gaining referrals from driving schools but if you include one of your leaflets with the letter you may get the instructor along for his nerves or backache.

Becoming a qualified driver also involves passing a written examination. For a few people the practical side of driving is easy but the written paper can be daunting. Some people will remember school days and how badly they did in their history or English papers, for example. If you have experience of working with any college students and helping them with their memory and recall abilities, you can use the same process with driving school pupils. Again, include details of feedback from past relevant client successes in your letter.

8

Health Connections Plus!

Any link that you can establish to orthodox health and other essential professions will bring many benefits, including enhancing clients' perceptions of trust and integrity.

(58) ADVERTISING IN HOSPITALS

A place that the general public may frequently visit is a hospital. People go there for their own medical problems, with someone else who needs to attend for treatment or because they are visiting a friend or relative who is a patient. Whatever the reason, many people pass through a hospital's doors.

You can promote your practice in an environment where people's minds are going to be focussed on their health. Just imagine a man who suffers with high blood pressure who is sitting in the patients' arrivals area and waiting to be called. He is wondering whether his blood pressure is going to improve or not. He may be on medication. He may have the opinion that medication is the only means of help, even with its side effects. Then he spots a poster offering a treatment that can help him to reduce his anxiety levels and to relax more. He might not take any action the first time he sees that poster, or the second, but at some point he will be tempted to find out more.

Likewise, outpatients who suffer with circulatory problems or breathing disorders are told that they must stop smoking. Despite this advice, many still carry on because they don't feel that they can stop without help. Then they notice some 'stop smoking' leaflets describing a service that can help them. There is a good chance that they will at least take the leaflet away with them and telephone you for more information.

In those hospital waiting rooms you have a captive audience. Those people are bored and are looking for things to occupy their minds. They are also anxious about their ailment. If your therapy can genuinely offer them hope, you will increase your chances of turning them into a client.

Places to distribute your leaflets

- Blood testing department

- X-ray

- Maternity wards and clinics

- Accident and Emergency departments

- Canteen and coffee areas

- Retail outlets

- Nurses' quarters

- Waiting areas

Go back to the hospitals on a regular basis to check on the posters you have put up on noticeboards and the leaflets you have distributed. You will probably need to replenish the supply of leaflets every two or three weeks.

(59) WORKING WITH THE EMERGENCY SERVICES

People who work for the emergency services are in the front line. Their roles involve dealing with horror, shock, violence or the results of violence. At some point in time, it takes its toll and these people can start to suffer from the effects of stress, which can reduce their ability to perform.

In any locality there are the fire services, ambulance services, and police departments. It would be rare to find an emergency service organisation that provides adequate support in the form of stress relief. The help tends to come only when someone has passed a point of no return.

Be proactive and offer your therapy to the local fire brigade. Arrange a couple of hours for a group therapy session or for short individual sessions. Involve the local newspaper to get free publicity, particularly if you are giving your services free. If the people you treat feel positive benefits, you can give them the opportunity to see you privately or give regular fortnightly or monthly group sessions. Charge a nominal fee per attendee for group sessions.

Managing your emergency services association

1. Make your service as easy as possible for them to use.
2. Get into the habit of always attending at the same time on the same weekday.
3. Get permission to put posters up in the building describing your therapy service.
4. Tailor your practice brochure to reflect how you can help the issues affecting this group of people and distribute them.
5. Ask for an article about you and your therapy to be included in the trade union's or organisation's newsletters.

Just think how impressive the title of 'Reflexologist to the Stanhope Fire Department' would be on your career record. It can also open other doors for you as far as work with organisations is concerned and you increase your chance of personal referrals through the fire station and new clients from the initial publicity of your first visit. Once you are established at one police station or fire station you can approach others with confidence.

60 ADVERTISING ON DOCTORS' APPOINTMENT CARDS

Clients who receive regular treatment from their doctor or a nurse are given appointment cards. The cards act as a reminder of the time and date of the next appointment and also give contact details of the surgery just in case the client needs to cancel and arrange a different appointment or for other queries.

Appointment cards are therefore looked at on a number of occasions by the patient and generally the patient brings the card with them to the surgery so that the next appointment can be added to it. The management of some surgeries have realised that they can generate income if they allow other services to promote their business via the cards. The smallest surgeries have around 5,000 patients and the largest can have upwards of 20,000, so the scope for your details being read by a patient is high. You could secure a reasonably prominent advertisement on the appointment card.

You could advertise on appointment cards that are given to people who have a particular ailment. These people are attending the surgery because they want to overcome that ailment. If you can also offer help with their condition, then they are likely to at least consider seeing you.

At first glance, it seems that this form of marketing could be quite rewarding. However, do be careful and do not sign up for any price. Remember that not all of the 20,000 patients will be given an appointment card, particularly if their visit is a 'one off'. Many patients will not be able to afford your fee, which in part is why they are seeing their doctor for help. Finally, if they are already receiving treatment they might wait to see if the conventional treatment has an effect before considering anything else.

61 REGISTERING WITH THE NATIONAL HEALTH SERVICE

Registering with the National Health Service (NHS) can add a perceived quality to your practice. Let it be clear that this does not signify any form of recognition by the NHS on the quality of your skills or your qualifications. The purpose of this registration, which involves being issued with an NHS number, is that you can obtain payment from the NHS for referred NHS patients.

This sounds as if all you have to do is accept any person who cannot afford to pay your fees as an NHS patient. In reality this is far from the truth. If the NHS is going to pay for a patient's treatment, they must be referred to you by their doctor. Even this is not enough because although the doctor might agree, the ultimate decision is made by whoever controls the NHS funds for the area. A doctor has to apply for funds to the local Health Trust. Only if the local trust agrees to pay for treatment will you be able to have the patient's treatment funded by the NHS.

These referrals tend to be few and far between, particularly because doctors remain uninformed about complementary therapies. However, registration with the NHS is free and seems to bring with it credibility from the client's point of view. A client who notices the phrase, 'NHS Provider Number G12345' on your brochure is more likely to trust your skills.

A similar situation exists regarding funding of complementary therapies through private health companies. In practice you can register with the private health companies. However, only patients who are referred to you by a company consultant will have their treatment paid by the health company. Clients who approach you directly and have private health care will not be able to get their treatment paid for just because you are registered. But again, stating that you have a private health company provider number adds to the kudos of your practice without costing you anything, as registration is free.

9

Networks

People are a therapist's most important resource, not only in terms of customers but in terms of marketing or spreading the word.

62 YOUR OWN 'BOARD OF ADVISORS'

Running your own business successfully often means using all the resources that you can get hold of without incurring unnecessary expense. In keeping with the expression, 'two brains are better than one' there is a way of taking advantage of this fact without going into partnership with anyone else.

Inviting active contributors

Invite about six friends, relatives or acquaintances to a dinner party at your home. Make it clear why you are inviting them and what you expect from them. In effect, you are paying for their ideas for your business by providing them with a free dinner.

Tell them that there will be other people at the dinner (whom they may or may not know) and you just want them to contribute some ideas to help your business. The majority of people invited will be flattered to think that you hold their opinions and ideas in such high esteem. This must be true, of course, because otherwise you wouldn't have invited them.

You must do your homework before inviting just anybody. You need your guests to be as productive as possible, so invite people who you really believe will make a useful contribution and not just those who are good company socially. Also, be clear about the areas of your business that you want them to focus on. Don't let them wander off the point.

Keeping the meeting focussed

If the main thrust of the evening is going to be how to increase the number of marketing strategies you use, then let them know in advance. When they arrive at the party they will then have already given it some prior thought. When the ideas start flowing, make a note of them. Don't leave them to memory.

If this function turns out well, then repeat it every few months or so. If some guests did not perform very well, substitute them at the next meeting. The advantage of this informal get together is that you are not offering anyone a position in your business. It is also easy for you to change guests at your whim. It can be good, of course, to have fresh blood anyway and not always invite the same people each time.

The cost to you is the food and drink you provide plus your time. The return is the benefit of having your own 'board of advisors' or think tank all focussing on advancing your business. You also gain contacts. Someone will always say something like, 'I know someone who's looking for a therapist who can help with . . .'. Encourage them all to take away business cards to pass on to anyone who is interested in your services.

Increasing your network

Take this time to find out about the clubs and societies they belong to and whether they would like you to give a talk about your therapy or whether they have a newsletter or bulletin board that your can advertise with. It is said that we all know approximately 200 people. By tapping into your board of advisors' contacts you increase your network several fold.

FORMING A CO-OPERATIVE

Once a therapist has qualified and starts their practice, they will at some point, start to feel isolated. This can be especially true if their previous career involved working for an organisation where they were part of a team. The usual camaraderie is no longer there; they are now the sole worker relying on their own decisions and opinions.

Reducing isolation

You can add to your marketing strategies armoury and help reduce feelings of isolation by forming a loose co-operative or network of therapists. The therapists can have different skills or offer a different type of service. For instance, in a co-operative you could have a homeopathist, herbalist, rolfer, NLP therapist, acupuncturist, reflexologist and others. No member should offer the same therapy as another. In other words, you would not have two aromatherapists because any referrals would have to be split between them.

The idea is that each therapist can refer their clients or potential clients to any of the therapists in the co-operative. Sometimes a client seeking help with a particular issue will telephone a therapist and want a personal recommendation for another form of treatment rather than picking anyone at random from the phone book. A crystal healer might refer an existing client or enquirer to the osteopath in the co-operative and truthfully assure the client that they know the therapist personally.

Forming your co-operative

To start the co-operative, simply look for advertisements or leaflets from local therapists and when you are ready, invite them to an informal meeting over a coffee. They will love the idea because there is no rivalry within the co-operative as no two therapists offer the same service. Meeting on a regular basis can help with reducing the isolation and is a great time to exchange ideas or plan other ventures together.

As long as everyone agrees, it can be supportive of this venture to have a supply of brochures from each member on display in all the individual practices, or at least a supply available to give to any interested client.

A client who has come to you for therapy through a personal recommendation is more trusting of you and will have more belief in your therapy skills. They will also feel safer and more secure in your practice because you are known to other practitioners and are not someone who has set up overnight.

(64) JOINING AN ASSOCIATION

Any therapist who takes their profession seriously should belong to an appropriate association. The association gives credibility to its members by stipulating that they have to be of a certain standard and must abide by a code of conduct. Any membership fees should be more than offset by the benefits you gain by belonging to an association. One of those benefits can be client referrals.

The number of client referrals you receive this way can vary dramatically. Some associations actively promote themselves in such places as every edition of the *Yellow Pages*. Any client who contacts them will be given details of the members in their area. Some associations have a separate marketing programme that you can join but for which you may have to pay an additional fee.

Whatever scheme your association uses you should expect at least an occasional client to be referred to you. You help this possibility by keeping in touch with the administrators of the membership. If they know your name and have spoken to you, they are more likely to suggest to an enquirer that you can help them.

Another way in which an association can help is by providing the opportunity for shared advertising. Therapists who belong to the organisation and are in the same geographical location can divide the expense of a *Yellow Pages* advertisement between them. The advert lists details of all the participating therapists (including names, designations and contact details) and that they all are members of the association. This stated relationship between therapist and association seems to increase the perception of professionalism and trust among the general public.

Many therapists return to their associations to seek their help when they want to run a workshop for other therapists. Often the association will allow its mailing list to be used to advertise the workshop and may even sponsor the event in some capacity.

Some therapists take out membership with several associations because the fees are more than covered by the benefits they receive.

65 BUILDING NETWORKS

If you use an accountant for bookkeeping and a lawyer for legal matters, make them a part of your network. They know your success gives them opportunity for more business from you. Supply them with a few business cards and encourage them to give you referrals. This works both ways, as you can give them referrals, particularly as you are likely to mix with other small business entrepreneurs.

More networking opportunities

How many other professional contacts do you have? When a plumber comes to fix your boiler, take his card and give him your business card. While you are waiting for him to do his job, tell him about your work and all the ailments you help with and the benefits your therapy provides. Do not assume that just because he has heard of your type of therapy he knows all about it. You can do the same with the post woman or the gas meter reader or any other service provider you come into contact with. These workers mix with the general public all the time and are bound to talk about you and your therapy because it is unusual.

Talk to the cashier at the bank and at the supermarket checkout. Pass pleasantries at the hardware store and at the bakers. Drop into the conversation what you do. When you tell people that you are a therapist they become immediately interested because it is still relatively unusual. Try to plant a seed in their mind by saying as you leave, 'Well, I must be going. If you know anyone who needs a massage, just send them to me'. There is a good possibility that the next time you see this person, they will say that they have been talking about you and their friend/relative/customer wants to come and see you. If you haven't already done so, now is your chance to give them a business card or six!

The cost to you is spending a few moments chatting. The rewards can be a regular flow of referrals.

Joining networking organisations

There are organisations that provide a more professional approach to networking. This involves paying an annual fee and meeting once a week. The meeting is usually for breakfast, for which there is another cost. The occasion involves participants making a two-minute speech about their service. Every member is encouraged to gain referrals for all other members. All referrals are monitored to see who has not only been getting referrals, but generating them. If you decide to join an organisation like this, you must commit yourself wholeheartedly to the process of selling yourself to fellow members and generating referrals to make the cost worthwhile.

66 USING MAILING LISTS

Marketing is about letting people know that you exist and persuading them that you can help with their problem or ailment. Many marketing methods use a scatter gun approach. This means that for every 10 people who you reach with your message, only three will need your service. Much of your effort can be wasted on those who do not need you (at least not immediately) if you are not careful.

Focussing your efforts

Using a mailing list can provide a target to aim for. Mailing lists are being constructed all the time with information about people's habits, lifestyle, likes and dislikes. Computer databases can allow for such complex manipulation of data nowadays that if you were only interested in contacting blue-eyed, bearded men who are deaf in one ear, then a mailing list could be produced for you. Every item that we buy indicates something about us and this information can be used to target us with offers of similar goods.

If a dietician wanted to attract overweight clients, a list of names and addresses could be purchased through a mailing list bureau. People who have back problems could be approached by a practitioner of Alexander Technique. Special offers could be sent to stress sufferers with a discount off a meditation course to help them relax more.

Once a mailing list has been purchased, you can then periodically send out details of your therapy. Gift vouchers, group sessions or special offers could be communicated this way.

Using the above approach, you can be reasonably confident that you are tapping into a warm market. A 'warm' market is when people have indicated that they have a need for your type of service.

If you use this strategy, be clear about the type of person you are looking for. Try to have the mailing list as focussed as you can get it. Remember, your geographical location is an important factor. It is no good setting up in Colchester and getting an address for someone in Glasgow if they need to attend your practice. Purchasing mailing lists can be quite expensive. Have a clear idea on the sort of return that you require to make it worthwhile.

BUILDING A DATABASE

Instead of buying a list of names and addresses to promote
your therapy you could build your own client database.
Once a person has sampled your therapy skills, even
though they may not book another session it does not
mean that they will never want your services again. Often
it is the case that their lives are so busy that they never get
round to contacting you again. They may even lose your
address and telephone details. How many times have you
accepted somebody's business card, only discover it is
missing when you need it?

Reminding clients about you

Mailing an occasional promotion to previous clients who
have not visited you for a while can reap rewards. Your
letter can often arrive at an appropriate time and many
people may see your letter as fate or perhaps they have
been intending to come for therapy again. Now that they
have your details once more they have the opportunity to
take up the offer or even pass it on to a friend.

You can even try the old marketing ploy of giving a
time-limited discount to encourage them to take action
now. This can be something like:

**Book your session before 31st March to
receive a free product sample or 10% discount.**

You can also use your database to keep private clients
informed of any classes or workshops you intend to run.
Likewise people who have attended one workshop of yours
should be notified of any new workshops you intend
running.

This strategy will not be appropriate to every therapy.
Psychotherapists, counsellors and hypnotherapists may feel
that it is not ethical to approach past clients in this way, but
for other therapists it may be quite acceptable.

114

JOINING LOCAL TRADING SCHEMES

There are a number of schemes that act like a network and encourage a form of bartering. In the UK there is a scheme called LETS (Local Enterprise Trading Scheme). This allows people who are members to trade goods and services using a fictitious currency called 'beams' (or other suitable name). Instead of hard cash passing hands, these 'beams' are used to pay for items.

The scheme helps people to offer goods for sale, skills, therapies and other commodities and their reward is to be paid an agreed amount of beams. They can in turn use the beams to purchase whatever they want from other members.

This doesn't help to pay your bills but it can save you money because in effect you are bartering your therapies for items you want. A newly qualified therapist might need a website for promotion purposes. The therapist offers their therapy to members for a set number of beams. Those beams can then be used to hire a web designer who is also a member the scheme. Each person decides how many beams they will charge for their services or goods.

All the LETS groups publish a newsletter at least once every three months and just like other newsletters are always looking for interesting articles. When you first join a LETS group, or even if you are a longstanding member, take the opportunity to promote your therapy by writing an interesting article. Give some tips about stress relief or goal achievement or some simple acupressure techniques, for example. The article should then say how much more can be gained by attending a session with you.

You wouldn't want to earn all your income in beams, but it is another useful way of networking.

69 EXCHANGING THERAPIES

As therapists we can appreciate the benefits of our own therapies because we see the evidence with our clients.

115

Sometimes though, when we apply the therapy to ourselves, it can be a bit like tickling your own feet: it may not be as powerful or as enjoyable.

Exchanging therapies gains more for you

With this in mind it can be wonderful to get together with other therapists in your area and exchange therapies. You could swap an acupuncture session for a reflexology session or kinesiology session for a meditation session. The benefits of this are that you gain experience of what another therapy is like and also how another therapist works. Also, because you now know another therapist through personal experience you will feel more confident about recommending them to people, and of course they will feel able to recommend you.

It is important to be clear about your exchange, swap or barter agreement with anyone. A Reiki therapist may charge £40 per hour while a Rosen body worker may charge £60 per hour. If these two therapists decide to swap their services, is it fair to exchange an hour of therapy or should the fee differences be taken into account? Usually, for simplicity's sake a straight swap will be agreed; one session of Reiki for one session of Rosen body work.

Unlimited benefits

Exchanging does not have to limit itself to fellow therapists. You could barter your services with a bricklayer or decorator or anyone who is agreeable to such an arrangement. The more people you treat with your therapy, the bigger your chances of your reputation spreading and attracting paying clients.

(70) MENTORING

I am sure most people have heard the expression 'why re-invent the wheel'. The lesson of this saying applies to your therapy practice in many ways. Instead of making mistakes that can cost you time, money and maybe your reputation, why not learn from someone else's mistakes?

Find someone who is a success at what they do. This person should ideally be providing the same therapy that you are skilled in and have a practice that you would like to have for yourself. In other words, they have achieved, or are well on their way to achieving, the type of thriving practice you dream of. By finding such a person, you support your confidence that your dreams can become your living reality because someone is already out there doing it. Secondly, you have found a perfect mentor.

Some successful therapists will not want to take on the responsibility of mentoring another therapist for a variety of reasons. The trick in getting someone to assume the role is not to make the 'mentor' title official. If you just ask for advice, the seasoned therapist will be happy to help because they may recall how they struggled initially and were helped by others. You should also use your mentor's time sparingly. You can still try things out for yourself and learn from your mistakes but you may want some guidance for the major decisions.

Try not to be a carbon copy of your mentor but incorporate your own style and aim to improve on your mentor's suggestions. There is, of course, nothing to stop you having more than one mentor.

10

Using Retail Outlets

It can be very rewarding to form loose partnerships with local traders of all varieties to increase your profile.

71 HAIRDRESSERS AND BARBERS

There is no doubt that personal recommendation is the best form of advertising for any business, not least because it is without cost. When people get together for any reason, they usually end up chatting about any subject from politics to sport, noisy neighbours to the family. Hairdresser and barber shops seem to provide an excellent environment for the passing of opinions, information and gossip not only by the customers but also by the staff.

When your hair is being cut, permed, washed or dyed there isn't a lot you can do to pass the time other than to talk. The staff realise that if they engage the customer in conversation it helps them to relax and enjoy their time there. The customer has opinions and will generally make them known. Furthermore, customers can hear other conversations and may offer a word of help or laugh with a joke.

Advice is free and most people like to pass on their 'pearls of wisdom' given the chance. The hairdresser's is also a place where people unburden themselves and start to talk about their problems.

From the therapist's point of view, this environment and the interactions that happen within its boundaries can provide a rich seam of clients. It only takes one customer to talk about your practice and suddenly many others are listening. People like to hear about the unusual and even though complementary and alternative therapy is becoming more popular, it is still considered something outside the norm and special. Therefore it is intriguing.

Even if a customer at the hairdresser's doesn't admit to needing help they can still be making a mental note and seek out your services at a later date.

All of the above will work as long as you have someone who talks about the therapy they received from you. Given the opportunity, they will do this, as long as their problem was not of a delicate or personal nature.

Tapping into a rich seam of clients

What can really help your marketing is if one of the hairdressers talks about your therapy. The hairdresser is in a position of influence and can be of great value to you. With this in mind, be proactive and seek their help. There are a number of tactics you can use. The direct approach of 'Will you recommend clients to me?' is unlikely to work unless they have sampled your therapy first hand.

You could offer one of the hairdressers a free session. This could be amply rewarded by any referrals. If it works out well you may even consider giving, in turn, each of the staff a free session.

Swapping a therapy session for a hair cut could be another way of getting your services known. This way you get something immediately for your services plus the prospect of referrals.

Gaining those clients

Another way is to leave some small leaflets at all the hairdressers in your locality. The manager of the establishment will, nine times out of ten, have no objection to you leaving some leaflets, particularly if you suggest they are for his or her clients. You can use wording like this:

'Hi, I am a local reflexologist (or aromatherapist or naturopath, etc.) . . . I just wondered whether I could leave a few leaflets for your clients?'

119

You will be amazed at how the staff can become very interested in you. They don't have many therapists coming to their door and you may find yourself being quizzed about your therapy. This shows that they are interested in you. They are not being hostile. Go to as many salons as you can and don't forget your own favourite place.

Every so often call back and refresh those leaflets. Tell them that some of your new clients have found out about you through them. They will feel good about helping you and be happy to take more leaflets.

You just need to say something like:

'I don't know if you remember me but I am the local reflexologist who left some leaflets here last month . . . Well, I just wanted to say, thanks very much because I've been able help some of your customers.'

As you leave, (as an after thought) say:

'Oh by the way, just in case you've run out, I thought I would drop in a few more leaflets.'

You will find very little objection and again you leave the staff of that business feeling good about themselves.

(72) SHOPS

An economical way of bringing your therapy to the attention of potential clients is advertising via your local shops. In its simplest form, you write on a postcard the details of what you are offering and a contact telephone number. Then you pay by the week for the card to be displayed in the shop window.

Rates vary but are still fairly low. This form of marketing will not appeal to everyone or be appropriate to the nature of every therapy. It would probably not work for the psychotherapist as the potential client may get the impression of someone who is not qualified or has little or no experience.

Yet for an aromatherapist, a more flexible perception of what is appropriate may be enjoyed. This is particularly so if the format of the advert elevates it above the surrounding mass of hand-written advertisements. If you decide to use this method, be creative. Use a different coloured card. Have the description typed or printed. State the benefits of your treatment but also include that you are professional, qualified and experienced. Include designations after your name to assist the air of professionalism.

Some shops will allow you to place a poster in the window. This gives you an even better chance to stand out from the run of the mill – bikes, furniture and other household goods for sale or wanted. You will probably be paying more for this but it could be worthwhile.

Be choosy about which shops you pick to advertise with. Opt for the most popular ones. You can easily spot these by watching the number of customers entering and leaving. Also watch out for the number of people who stop to read the notices in the window. Set a trial period for this option to see whether it will work for you.

(73) CAFÉ MENUS

Cafés, and smaller restaurants are places where people meet and talk on a regular basis. Families, friends and even individuals will often drop into a place to get something to eat or drink or both.

This is a chance to attract more clients and to do it in a way that builds a good relationship with local eating establishments. It will not cost you the earth and yet you can secure advertising all year round.

Spotting an opportunity
All these eating places have one thing in common – a menu. In these establishments the customers always scan

the menu. Even if they know what they want, they will look through the menu just to see if there is anything else of interest. This is your opportunity to increase your profile and with little cost.

Approach the manager or owner of the café and offer to provide them with new menus once a month. By menus, I mean the sheets of paper or cardboard that detail the different dishes and not the plastic outer coating or fancy folder (if there is one). You offer to do this for the café owner for free.

Give to get

You arrange to have the menus printed (on your computer or a borrowed one). This is your cost. In return, you get to advertise your therapy on the menu. You will need to negotiate how much space you can take up. If you choose a smallish café of about 12 to 20 tables, the print costs should be no more than £5 per month. That is £5 per month to have your business benefits in front of potential customers every time that café is open.

The café owner benefits by getting clean new menus at least once a month and getting a chance to change the meals or prices or both. The owner could more easily run special meals for different seasons as well as for Easter and Christmas. The owner gets this for free as part of the agreement.

A variation on the above is to provide business cards which sit in an attractive container on each table instead of printing your practice details on the menu. This is another way of bartering services – and your printing costs can still be claimed as a legitimate business expense.

(74) BEAUTY AND HEALTH SHOPS

A place where people think about how good they look and feel is a beauty parlour or health shop. These places are great for finding more paying clients.

Utilising available resources

A number of possibilities await you. Some of these establishments will have a spare room that is being under-used, if it is used at all. Approach the manager and suggest the idea of running a part-time service from that room.

The benefits for the shop are that they get some rent from your use of the room. They also get the chance to sell more of their services or products to your clients. Once the backroom is fit for use, the shop manager may invite other therapists to use it on the days that you do not.

With this arrangement, you get another place to practice and, because it is in the interest of the shop for you to succeed, they will help to get clients for you. The best arrangement (from your point of view) is to pay rent by the hour and only when you use the room. In other words, you only pay rent when you have a client. If you don't get this agreement, do think seriously about whether to walk away from this shop or not. Remember that if you pay rent whether you have clients or not, then the shop manager does not have any incentive to attract clients for you because whatever happens they still get their rent.

Increasing your chances of success

Encourage the shop owner to display your practice brochures in a good place in the shop. If you produce an A5 size leaflet giving details of your therapy, you might also persuade the shop owner to enclose one of these with items bought by the customer. If you can get permission, place a good sized poster (minimum A4) giving details of your service in the shop window. Include your own telephone number on the poster, thereby increasing your chances of gaining business even when the shop is closed.

SHOPPING CENTRES, PRECINCTS AND MALLS

Whenever you plan to have a 'blitz' on marketing it is useful to consider all the places where people congregate, visit or pass through for whatever reasons. A shopping centre of any size has people passing through it every day. The busiest day is usually a Saturday.

Think back to the last time you visited such a place and remember what happened as you went from store to store. Eventually, somewhere someone would have tried to thrust something into your hand. They might have been inside the shopping complex or standing outside, but there would have been at least one person doing this – if not several.

Stop me and take one

Companies, small and large do this type of marketing for a reason. It must bring in customers for them. If it works for them it can work for you. If you don't have the nerve to do it yourself, or don't want to be seen handing leaflets out, get a friend to do it or pay someone to stand there for you. It might prove to be a waste of time, but on the other hand it might be that winning strategy that you will want to use on a regular basis.

Do not use your most expensive leaflets or brochures. The majority of these will end up as rubbish. Make up an A5 size flyer from 80gsm paper and emphasise the problems you can help with. Your contact telephone number should be large but the name of your practice or your own name should be smaller. Highlight the words that attract people such as, FREE, DISCOUNT, SPECIAL OFFER, etc. If you give a free initial consultation, make sure this is mentioned and highlight benefits before features of your treatment.

Useful research

Before putting together your flyer, start to collect other flyers and see how they are designed. It will prevent elementary mistakes and enable you to make an impact the first time.

Check out the different shopping centres in your locality. Some will provide a better response than others. Make a list of those centres in the order that you feel would give you the best response. If you are going to stand inside the building you should check with the management to make sure that they have no objection to this. If you stand outside the centre on public land and hand your flyers out, there will generally be little problem.

Decide a set number of flyers to hand out at each centre and when this has been reached, move on to the next one. Depending on the distance, you may only be able to cover two or maybe three shopping centres in any one day. At each location start handing out your flyers as soon as you arrive.

Don't be put off by anyone who refuses to take a flyer or immediately throws it away. Every person you see who is not interested in your therapy means that you are that much closer to someone who is.

Don't expect the telephone to ring constantly because some people keep these flyers for months or even years before acting on them. If anyone asks you questions, do give them your time, as it shows that they are interested.

76 SPECIALIST SHOPS

With the popularity of 'New Age' ideas and spirituality today, you can find many shops that specialise in selling books, tapes, crystals, stones, etc. People who spend their money in these shops are likely to be more open and accepting of your therapy.

Join forces to increase success
Forming an alliance of some sort with such a shop may prove to be a very useful strategy. Sometimes these shops have noticeboards where therapists are encouraged to leave leaflets and business cards. These get swamped and

so you may find the leaflet you pinned up one day is under a pile of others the next day. You will get more consistent results (new clients) from this type of shop by having a closer connection.

Use your creative skills to put together a scheme that will benefit you and the shop. That should not be difficult. If you are a crystal healer, you could offer sessions from the shop for half a day a week. You get paid by the customers who are directed to you by the shop. The shop takes a percentage of your earnings for providing the space, and also earns from people who want to buy their own crystals.

You could negotiate a similar arrangement so that any customers enquiring about seeing a crystal healer will be given your business card or leaflet. Likewise, you can recommend to clients that they get their crystals from that shop. Another example of this arrangement is for an aromatherapist to team up with a shop that sells oils, candles, and incense burners.

With this arrangement everybody wins. The customer gets what they want: the therapy. The shop gets what they want: rent from the space you use and increased sales. You get paying clients in the shop and referrals to your private practice.

(77) SUPERMARKETS

The larger supermarkets are offering ways for local businesses to reach local customers. Next time you do your weekly shop, have a look at the back of the receipt. You may find all different types of local businesses advertising their products and services.

Before committing yourself to this type of advertisement you will need to be clear on how well it works for those who have already used it. Telephone any company that you find on the back of a receipt and ask them. If the business is a small one, like yours, most of the time they won't mind just giving a rough idea of its success. The ultimate test of whether it is a good promotion medium is whether they would renew their contract with the supermarket.

You will also need to find out how long the contract runs for and the geographical location of the supermarkets that will use till receipts with your advert. You don't want to pay for something with a wide coverage, most of which would be of little benefit to you.

Another way of making yourself known to the throngs of people that pass through your local supermarket is to check out their customer information area. Sometimes they provide a customer noticeboard. This is where customers can place notices to sell unwanted items or state what they are looking for. It can also be a place for you to place a small notice about your therapy.

Some supermarkets and some large hardware chains are providing a business card dispenser service. This is simply a facility for local businesses to provide a supply of business cards for customers to take. There is a charge for this service. You can choose to go in one store, or a number of them, in your location. It is better to try one store at a time to gauge the likely success of this medium. The position of the dispenser is very important. People are naturally lazy and won't go out of their way to look at it. Check those in your local stores and pick a store where virtually all customers pass by the dispenser. One of the better positions is after customers have paid for their goods and as they are leaving the store.

(78) WORKING IN A CAFÉ

Local cafés need to attract a regular clientele as well as passing trade. As with other establishments, it is the regular customers that keep a business healthy. A café needs to persuade customers that not only are their coffees, cappuccinos and other beverages superior to those that you could make at home but that they get other benefits too. Rather than being a place just to drink coffee and chat with friends, some cafés are extending their attractiveness.

More than just coffee

Lately, coffee and computers have come together to form internet cafés. With book shops now offering fresh coffee some cafés are turning the tables and displaying a range of books for sale that customers can browse through at their leisure whilst enjoying their coffee.

You can assume that café owners are open to new and exciting additions to their service. Here is an opportunity for the creative therapist. What service could you offer to the café's customers?

Any therapy you propose for this environment needs to take into account that it is a public place and privacy cannot be assured. There will usually be limited space in a café, so your therapy must not take up much room, or be disruptive to customers who just want to enjoy a chat and a coffee.

Ideas for therapists

- Reflexologist – could work on people's hands rather than their feet.

- Massage therapist – could provide Indian head massage.

- Nutritionist – could advise on suitable vitamins and minerals.

- Crystal therapist – could offer a re-balancing service.

Give a flavour only

All of the above should be short versions of the full therapy. Your aim is to give a flavour of the therapy and not a full session. You can charge a nominal amount for a short session. The cost should be small enough to allow customers to make an easy decision to buy but large enough to make it worth your while. If you build up a good relationship with the café owner before you propose any of the above services, you should be able to negotiate a fair agreement for your use of the café. Some café owners recognise that you are making the café a more attractive place and that word of mouth will bring more customers in. These customers will spend their money in the café and so you may not be charged anything for your use of one table.

To build a regular clientele and to let new clients find you, it is best to have a set day and time that you will make yourself available at the café. Have a notice put up in the café window publicising your service. Always bring plenty of brochures and business cards and your appointment diary with you.

11

The Internet

Technology is forever changing. The long-term successful therapist keeps up to date with changes in any areas that can affect the practice in a positive or negative way.

(79) CREATING YOUR OWN WEBSITE

You must set up your own website because one thing is for sure – your competitors will. Having a website is another part of a successful marketing strategy. Without a website and at the very least an email address, you might be viewed as outdated and this perception may reflect on the therapy you offer.

Setting up a website

There are many ways of putting together a website that even the absolute novice can tackle. Many therapists barter their services for something they want. Usually you will find someone in your circle of family and friends who will be a self-made expert on the internet and will have already put together their own website. Why not barter some of your therapy sessions to get your website built?

Alternatively you may decide to employ a web design bureau to put together a slick site and handle the technical details and registrations. At some point in time you will need to take control of your site and not leave it entirely to the bureau. It is better to get involved at the start.

If you fancy the idea of tackling this yourself, website building software is often given away with computer magazines. In fact all the software you require can be obtained for the cover price of those publications.

The name of the most popular code for a web page is HTML. This stands for HyperText Markup Language. Fortunately it is quite easy to understand. A great and easy way to get a quick understanding of how to code a web page is to copy an existing site from the Internet and then just play around with the code in a word processor. By doing this you will be able to see what the coding does and the effects you can achieve. This is a learning exercise only – you should not copy someone else's site and publish it as your own website as you will fall foul of copyright laws.

Your website address

Nothing beats having your own domain name that reflects the business you are in. However, initially you can make do with a free site package. These will still allow you to display the important information about you and your services. The drawback is that the address of the free site tends to be long and not so easy to remember, such as:

www.cheapserve.homeusers.com/commerce/therapy.htm

as opposed to the simplicity of your own domain name like:

www.great-therapy.com.

Once you have an email address and a website, include these details on all of your business paperwork. It provides a different way for people to get hold of you. Another advantagae is that people can retain a sense of anonymity while emailing you and asking questions which they don't get with the telephone. This can encourage potential clients to find out more about you and reduce their fears.

Dealing with the doubters

Your site can also help with people's objections by having a page dedicated to frequently asked questions (referred to as 'FAQs'). Just consider the top 20 questions that you get asked about your therapy and then list these questions with the answers. This can save you a lot of time.

Designing your site

Your website must be interesting, pleasant to the eye and easy to navigate. Do not use a multitude of colours. Choose three or four colours and use them consistently. For example, choose a deep blue for the background, white text and bold yellow for headings. There is always a temptation to use too many images. Images take time to appear and will slow down the loading of your page. If a web page takes too long to display visitors will get bored and move on to another site.

Your site must be slick, fast and to the point. Moving around your site from page to page should be easy and all the obvious information should be clearly accessible. There is a term in website design circles called being 'sticky'. This means that if you have a good site, your visitors will stick around and may even come back for more. If it is not sticky any visitor will move off very quickly and usually within the first 20 seconds. You literally have less than half a minute to make a good impression!

Make it as easy as possible for any Internet surfer to contact you. Display your telephone number and email address on every page of your website.

(80) REGISTERING WITH SEARCH ENGINES

Having a website that gives details of your therapy is a step forward but that is not the end of what you can do to promote yourself. Consider how people find information on the internet. The majority will use a search engine. You must get your site listed on these search engines.

There are hundreds of search engines. You could waste a lot of time trying to get listed on every search engine. This strategy would not be as rewarding as choosing to get listed on the most popular search engines.

Popular search engines

- www.yahoo.com

- www.altavista.com

- www.magallen.com

- www.excite.com

- www.go.com

- www.hotbot.com

- www.infoseek.com

- www.lycos.com

- www.google.com

All search engines provide on-line forms for you to submit your site for listing. However, just because you submit your site this does not mean that it will be listed. You will need to obey certain criteria. These will usually be stated when you fill the submission form out.

Once your site has been submitted, you must keep checking on its progress. There are software packages that will do this job for you. These generally form part of a web promotion deal that internet companies are now offering. There are web promotion sites that offer these services for free and will even provide a mini critique of your site and its coding.

Certain elements of the coding of your web page will either add or subtract from your ranking position in the search engines. Each search engine may use a slightly different set of criteria to decide which sites should be placed higher in the rankings. Generally, though, the following elements are important.

Keywords

These are words that web surfers will use in search engines to describe what they want to find. If you are a herbalist, some of the keywords a surfer may use to find you are:

herbalist, herbalism, herbs. These keywords need to be mentioned in the narrative of your first page at least five times. For some search engines you will need to mention the keywords more than this and others less. There is also a line of HTML code for you to state what your keywords are. The coding looks like this:

```
<META name="KEYWORDS" content= "herbalist,
herbalism, herbs">
```

You can include as many keywords as you want within the coding above. It may be useful to include your city or town and country. In this case the coding would like this:

```
<META NAME="KEYWORDS" content= "herbalist,
herbalism, herbs, london, england">
```

ALT tags

These are descriptions of any images that you have included in your website design. The idea is that if the internet surfer cannot see images, for whatever reason, they will get a description of the image instead. The description, known as an ALT tag, can be packed with keywords to help your search engine ranking. The coding for this would be:

```
<img src="home.jpg" ALT="London Herbalism from
an Experienced Herbalist">
```

NB home.jpg is the name of the image file.

Description

This part of the website tells the search engine about the content of your site. What you place here is often used when the results of a search are displayed to the surfer. When performing a search engine enquiry, you are usually shown the first ten websites with their addresses (URL) and a description for each site. It is the description of a site that will encourage a surfer to go to that site or not. Make your description short and to the point. Include the benefits of your therapy and any USP (Unique Selling Proposition) like a free initial consultation. The coding for a description would be:

<META NAME="DESCRIPTION" content= "Herbalism to help you resolve your problems such as fears, stress, pain, IBS and much more. Enjoy a free initial consultation from a London based Herbalist">

Notice that the opportunity has been taken to pack in three more keywords, which will again help your search engine ranking.

Title

This is simply the title that you give to your website. You should use this coding as another opportunity for repeating your keywords. Although search engine algorithms change, generally your title should have around five words in it. The first few words should repeat your keywords. The coding for this is:

<title>Herbalism by a London Herbalist</title>

Avoid spamming

Some people who code their own websites make the mistake of packing their pages with their keywords. This is called spamming. They make the text colour the same as the background colour in order to hide hundreds of keywords. The surfer is unable to see these keywords but the search engine is able to detect them. This may have worked at one time but now the search engines are able to recognise the deliberate proliferation of keywords and will no longer rank sites coded this way.

Monitor your website ranking

Web design companies will program and publish your site and will submit them to the search engines for you. This does not guarantee that you will either be accepted by the search engines or achieve a high ranking. Taking an interest in the coding of your website and using the examples above, will enable you to play an active role in achieving a better ranking and ultimately lead to more visitors to your site. Even when you have managed to appear in the top 50 websites for your keyword, you will still need to monitor your position and at intervals submit your site again. If a website's content remains the same for too long, the search engines will assume that it may not be as relevant and start to let it drop down the rankings. Keep your content fresh for the surfers and for the search engines and you will maintain its popularity.

(81) GETTING LISTED IN ON-LINE DIRECTORIES

There are other ways of getting your website known to prospective clients. Just as we have the *Yellow Pages* for telephone listings, so there are numerous directories on the Internet that list different services.

Yellow Pages also has a presence on the internet, as do other organisations who list any and every type of company and service. There are a number of on-line business directories that are worth investigating and obtaining a listing with. If you want to find these directories, simply type 'directories of services' or a similar description into any search engine.

Apart from general directories that list anything and everything, there are also specialised or niche directories which concentrate solely on particular types of services. These include website directories purely for alternative therapies. At the time of writing quite a few exist already and if you have a website up and running you will no doubt be approached by some of them. To actively seek a listing in these directories, type into the search engines 'therapy directory' or 'health directory'.

Some web directories

- www.SelfGrowth.com
- www.healthypages.co.uk
- www.uktherapists.com
- www.synergy-health.co.uk
- www.chisuk.org.uk
- www.goodhealthdirectory.com

If you can obtain a free entry with these niche directories then do take the opportunity. However, some of them will only list your business for a monthly or annual fee. If you pay for an entry with any and every directory that offers you the chance to be included, you will find your marketing budget soon runs dry and for little reward. Some prospective clients will find you through such schemes but do not expect to be deluged. In fact, because so many on-line directories exist and more are being created your return per website could be quite poor.

If one directory takes off and gains a solid reputation, then it would be worth considering parting with some of your marketing budget. Until and unless that happens you would be well advised to stay with the free entry offers.

82 PRODUCING ON-LINE ARTICLES

Just as national and local newspapers are hungry for interesting news items to fill their pages, so websites are hungry for appropriate articles to keep their visitors happy.

Often the alternative therapy directories will be more than a simple directory and include information on the therapies listed. As a result the website manager will be looking for therapists to provide articles on the services they offer, ailments that can be helped, an explanation of a particular ailment and how it can be treated, or even anonymous case histories.

There is nothing to stop you regurgitating articles you have had published elsewhere for this medium. Often they will be looking for an article of no more than a thousand words. Anything longer than that and the visitor becomes bored. Keep any composition relevant, short and snappy. Always get a link to your email or website from the article. This should be a standard agreement between you and the directory's webmaster.

Usually, once a month or so, the webmaster will want to put up a fresh article. If you are willing to provide fresh material you could find yourself becoming an editor for the site and gaining more exposure for your practice. In addition, many deleted articles will be placed in an archive area, so there are possibilities of attracting clients even though your article is no longer current. That is something you cannot say about a newspaper. Once the next edition is published, previous editions are not as easy to retrieve unless you visit the newspaper offices or a library or on-line archive.

(83) PARTICIPATING IN NEWSGROUPS

Usenet, which is simply an abbreviation of 'users network', is one of the world's biggest bulletin board systems. This facility enables the internet's millions of users to talk to like-minded people.

For example, anyone who is a Rosen method bodyworker or is thinking of visiting a Rosen method bodyworker or is just curious about it, can share information. Potential clients can ask questions and have them answered by experienced therapists. Therapists in turn may ask questions of their colleagues and get a number of opinions from different professionals. It is purely a way of exchanging views and opinions, asking questions, getting answers, to inform and be informed.

Generally the newsgroup operates via email messages. Someone sends in a message and then anyone can respond to it. Responses are organised in 'threads' so that they link back to the original email. This way anyone can sift through all the answers to a question posed by any single email.

If you play an active role by giving advice or just providing information on your area of expertise, you can build up a healthy reputation for yourself. If, when you respond to any email, you also include details of your website, you will attract surfers and new clients. There is no cost to join a newsgroup other than your time but the reward can be more clients.

(84) USING INTERNET CHAT ROOMS

Another way of communicating with potential clients is to visit a chat room on the internet. This is more immediate then a newsgroup because people who visit chat rooms are on line while they air their opinions or questions and you can respond to them immediately.

Unlike with newsgroups, the messages in the form of questions, views and responses are not archived but are lost once the user leaves the chat room. However, just like newsgroups each chat room has a particular subject or group of like-minded individuals. There may also be a geographical slant to the chat room. So a room can be for users based in New York who want to chat about psychotherapy. You can see that location and subject are quite important to a therapist who is trying to attract some of the chat room participants to their therapy practice.

You are able to be anonymous in chat rooms by choosing any alias before starting to chat. Instead of using your proper name you may want to be identified by a nickname such as 'UK_Iridiologist'. There is an etiquette called 'netiquette' which you must obey if you are to use chat rooms. This is no different to the professional code of conduct that you would follow normally in your practice anyway.

Using chat rooms can enable you to develop a following and help your reputation. Try to choose a regular time or day that you participate in the chat room. This will help any potential clients to find you more easily as your fame spreads.

85 ADVERTISING ON BANNERS

Look at any commercial website and you will notice advertisements for other companies and their products. These can appear anywhere on the site and in many forms. One of the more popular forms is a banner advertisement.

A banner is, as the name suggests, a rectangular space that contains details of a company's products or services. Its purpose is to tempt the visitor to click on the banner. Once this is done, the visitor is taken directly to that company's website.

Banners are a means of bringing visitors to your site, who may turn into paying clients. Given that there are millions of websites that offer banner advertising, you know logically that it would be time consuming and financially unrewarding to take up every offer. However, if you choose your sites carefully, it can be possible to attract a reasonable number of visitors to your site this way. Once they have arrived at your site, it is then up to you to encourage them to stick around and become a client.

There are two ways of arranging to have banner advertising on other sites. One is simply paying a fee. The other is a banner exchange. You place their banner on your site and they will place yours on theirs. The arrangement is likely to be a 'two for one' or 'three for one' agreement. This means that you will need to have two or three banners on your site advertising someone else's wares but you will only be allowed one banner on their site.

As you may gather, if you are not careful your site can end up covered in banners and will lose its appeal to any visitors. If you decide that banner advertising is for you, try not to have more than two per page.

86 SWAPPING LINKS

Internet users find what they are looking for, in the majority of cases, by using the search engines. When you type in a subject in any search engine you will be presented with thousands, if not millions, of websites. If your site is not listed in the top 50, there is little chance of getting a steady stream of visitors. Research has shown that Internet users rarely go beyond the top 50 sites.

There are a number of ways of improving your search engine ranking and one of them is by increasing your link popularity. Search engines use various algorithms to calculate which sites should have the best positions. A site that has a lot of other websites linked to it is considered to be more relevant and of interest. Therefore the search engines will place a site with many relevant links higher in the rankings.

Go to any website and 99% of the time you will find a 'links' page. This is simply a web page that contains links to other (usually relevant) sites. You click on the link and are taken directly to that website. This adds a quality to the site and shows that it also offers useful information and connections to other resources. The visitor will be grateful for these links and may even return to your site often because of the useful links you have. Of course, every time they return to your site, for whatever reason, it increases the possibility of turning them into a paying customer.

Adding relevant links

Among the smaller business community, links are often swapped. A bit like, if you put details of my website on yours, I will put your details on mine. A therapist in Swansea may swap links with someone in Cardiff or have an international links page and swap with a therapist in Washington DC, USA or Sydney, Australia.

The more relevant links you have between like-minded businesses the more points you score with the search engines and the higher your ranking will be. The higher your ranking, the more visitors you will attract to your website.

Getting more links

The best way of achieving good links is to approach other therapists, health retailers and businesses directly. Go to their sites and find out if they have a links page. If they do, email them and ask them to swap links. Make it as easy as possible for them by including the description that you want to have and also, if you can, the HTML code. If you have an attractive site it would be unusual for you to be turned down. In the unlikely circumstance that you are turned down, just move on to other sites. There are millions of websites out there and the numbers increase by thousands each day.

 USING EMAIL LISTS

Many marketing or web promotion organisations are offering ways of reaching potential clients by using emails. Anyone whose email address is known to the organisation can be sent details of your services via their email address.

Generally there are two options involved in this strategy. The first is to provide the marketing company with details of your sales pitch. State in less than 50 words what you are offering and how you can be contacted. The company will then include these details on a mail shot to a set number of addresses. Your costs will probably be calculated by the number of people you choose to emailed.

The second option is for you to purchase in advance a set number of email addresses and also to purchase a multi-mailing software package. You can then email those addresses as many times as you want with your offers. The multi-mailing software makes the task easy and quick.

With both choices you reach a lot of people very quickly but much of this type of mail is considered to be junk mail or email 'spamming'. Email spamming (sending unsolicited emails) is becoming more and more frowned upon and may even become illegal. Most marketing companies therefore are now offering a list of addresses where the owners have opted to receive special offers. This is one step better than spamming but much of what is sent this way will still be considered as junk mail and deleted quickly, often without it even being read.

Focussing is more rewarding

The better option is to obtain a list of email addresses from individuals who have shown a definite interest in your type of services. Purchasing a mailing list of people who are interested in alternative or complementary medicine will be more rewarding than a list of just anyone's email address. The more focussed your address list, the more you increase your chances of attracting new customers.

Don't be tempted by those websites professing to have the facility to email 10,000,000 addresses for you. You will be wasting your time, effort and money.

88 PROVIDING INTERNET THERAPY

Some holistic practitioners, particularly the 'talk' type therapies, will be able to offer a new dimension to their practice: providing therapy via the Internet.

For life coaches, NLP practitioners, hypnotherapists, psychotherapists and others the internet provides a means of reaching a wider catchment area. Considering that the Internet is available globally, there are now no boundaries (as far as location is concerned) to whom you can help. Web cameras (known as web cams) costing anything from £30 upwards are enabling businesses to utilise video conferencing. Meetings can be held in different countries and connected together by video. People at the meeting can be seen and heard.

For the therapist with an eye for the latest technological developments, this can mean that their client base is no longer restricted to a town or city but can be national and even international. With certain therapies, extra precautions will be necessary to ensure the safety of the client. But who is to say that life coaching, counselling and the like can not be successful via a video link?

If you physical therapists are feeling left out . . . don't be! There is always the possibility of teaching classes via a video link. A reflexologist could teach the basics to the husband, who then practises those strokes on his wife under the watchful gaze of the practitioner via the web cam. Classes of twos, threes or fours could be organised in Sydney, Australia with the tutor based in London, for example. The possibilities are endless and only limited by your imagination.

If you are going to offer your therapy to a national and international audience, you will need to consider how you will be paid. Cheques and cash will not be appropriate. With a few exceptions (schemes like Pay Pal) credit cards will be your main method of accepting payment. Before offering your therapy outside of your town or city get a facility for accepting credit cards. It is worthwhile shopping around for this service and not just accepting your own bank's rate because costs can vary quite substantially. If you are going to take payment via credit card on the internet, you will need to make sure that the customers' details are secure from hackers. Specialist companies provide such facilities.

12

Extra Enticers

Get past people's doubts and objections and you stand a better chance of turning an enquirer into a customer.

(89) REWARDING RECOMMENDERS

As you become more and more established you will find that word starts to spread about how good you are. You will find people telephoning you for an appointment because a previous client has recommended you. This method of obtaining new clients is essential for any long-term business.

Personal recommendations are important because any business needs to build a solid reputation for the service it provides. A client who has been referred to you by someone else has more faith in your abilities than in a therapist who has been picked randomly from some directory. In effect they have had proof that you can get results, otherwise you would not have been recommended.

As the therapist, you have not had to spend any of your income on marketing to get this person as your client. This client arrives with the belief that because they know someone you have helped, you can help them also.

Some unique therapists are able to brag that they never advertise for clients and that all their clients find them through their reputation. This is an enviable position to be in, but for the majority of therapists word of mouth alone is unlikely to provide a sufficient number of callers. People who are willing to recommend you should be encouraged.

Take the opportunity to talk to your clients about the other ailments you can help, for example, backache. If that client then sees a friend or relative who has backache they are likely to talk about your service. If a past client sends you a number of new clients, do find a way of rewarding them. This could be as simple as paying them a referral fee per client, or you may decide to offer them a complementary session as a gesture of thanks. Even just a short letter thanking them for their efforts can be enough to encourage them to continue referring people to you. Every referred client enhances your reputation and reduces your marketing costs.

(90) OFFERING DISCOUNTS

Never restrict yourself with your marketing ideas. If the large companies have a new way of encouraging people to try their product, play with the idea and see if you can copy their concept for your business.

Some clients will book an occasional therapy session every month or so. Others will want a series of sessions. It can be useful to know in advance how many clients you have next week, next month and even over the space of a year. Discounts can encourage the client to make definite dates for future sessions rather than coming on an ad hoc basis.

There are many strategies for making discounts work for you and numerous schemes to offer. The best for your practice may be the tried and tested favourite of 'pay for five sessions in advance and get the sixth free'. This scheme means that you have payment before any sessions start and have future sessions booked. Another option is to give an existing client a discount voucher (e.g. 10% off) for a friend or relative or to encourage your clients to recommend you to others and reward them with discounts for every new client they send to you.

If you give out discount vouchers, always have a 'use by' date on them. This helps the potential client to make up their mind to use your services sooner rather than later. It also means that you don't have hundreds of discount vouchers floating around that may turn up years later when you no longer need to use this strategy.

You may also consider giving discounts to specific groups of people. For example, you could offer anyone who works for the NHS a special Health Service discount. This focussed discount strategy can help raise your profile amongst doctors, nurses and others in the caring professions.

(91) SELLING GIFT VOUCHERS

As you might expect with this strategy, you simply sell gift vouchers that can be exchanged for therapy. This will not be applicable to certain therapies such as hypnotherapy or psychotherapy. If a friend or relative bought you a gift voucher to be redeemed at a psychotherapist's practice, you would consider it odd to say the least.

Selling gift vouchers will be more applicable for those such as aromatherapists, reflexologists, colour healers and others – if you like, the more physical type therapies, as opposed to the mental and emotional therapies.

As with discount vouchers, always have a 'use by' date. It would be considered fair to make the gift voucher valid for one year. Certainly other businesses such as book sellers issue gift certificates with a similar 'use by' date.

In your practice room have a display of gift vouchers and mention this in your practice brochure. You may even suggest to your clients that an excellent and unusual Mother's Day gift is the chance to enjoy a wonderfully relaxing massage.

The only cost to you is the printing of the gift voucher. The advantages are that you get paid in advance whether the recipient uses the voucher or not. It is also a great way of increasing your client base and often the person who has been treated to a therapy will want to pay for more sessions themselves.

Just like vouchers you can buy from booksellers, the gift voucher looks better if it is presented in a blank greetings card. The blank card allows the person giving the gift the space to write a personal message. You can charge a nominal amount for the card and envelope. This extra touch of providing cards and envelopes shows that you have given consideration to the presentation of the gift voucher to the recipient and adds to your client's perception of your professionalism.

92 OFFERING A FREE INITIAL CONSULTATION

Although many people will consider booking a session with you, a large percentage of these people will do nothing about it. They may take your leaflet and say to themselves that they will think about it later but never actually follow through and book an appointment. In effect they have what is known in marketing circles as an objection.

An objection is just something that stops them from going ahead and paying for a session (or service or product, etc.). They have a question or two which they would like to have answered before they will feel more comfortable about proceeding. A way of getting past that objection is to offer all your clients a free initial consultation.

A free consultation gives potential clients a chance to come along and meet you and ask their questions. They are not paying for this time and so they know that they have nothing to lose except their time. Although questions can be asked over the telephone or via email, people generally will not feel happy about parting with their money until they have met you in person and have those answers.

This does not necessarily apply to all therapies. It tends to be more relevant to talk therapies and particularly for help with mental and emotional issues. Having said that, not all 'talk' therapists offer a free consultation. Some will charge for it. Often it is down to the therapist's personal choice. For the physical therapies, you will very rarely have to offer a free consultation. This strategy tends to be used by the new therapist to encourage the 'ditherers' to make up their mind. Once a client is sitting in front or you, and as long as you do not make a silly mistake, the majority will proceed into therapy after the consultation.

Reserving the next hour

For some therapists a successful strategy with free consultations is to make the following hour available so that the client can start their therapy straightaway. If the client leaves after the consultation because you do not have the space in your appointments to start their first session, you risk the possibility of losing them and wasting the time that you gave them. Alternatively, by reserving an hour and a half for a client (e.g. consultation plus therapy session) you also risk them leaving after 30 minutes and wasting the following hour which you had kept clear just in case they wanted to proceed. Expect to lose time or clients no matter which strategy you use. You will find out the best procedure for you through trial and error.

Decide how long your free consultation will be and stick to it. Thirty minutes seems to be the popular choice. If you decide to keep the following hour free for your client make them aware of this before they arrive. If you inform them of this choice they are more likely to come prepared to take advantage of it. Using this method you will deal with any objections and it can become a USP (Unique Selling Proposition) for your practice.

93 GIVING FREE TALKS

Do not be afraid to provide free talks to the local community. Your library will sometimes have a room that they will let you use, or a community centre will allow you to provide free educational talks on the benefits of your therapy.

At schools, take the opportunity to talk to pupils who are looking for a career. Schools always invite the accountants, computer programmers and engineers to talk about their careers, so take advantage of this opportunity and talk about your occupation. Tell them about your business and the fun you have. Provide leaflets for them to take away. Also give mini demonstrations if you want them to get a flavour of your therapy. You will stick out like a sore thumb and be the talk of the school. Details of your talk and the therapy you offer will spread beyond the school gates and teachers to the parents.

This type of marketing costs you only your time and requires no expense other than the production of some extra leaflets. It increases your public persona and gets you talked about. New clients would rather see a therapist that they have heard something about (unless it is negative) than have to pick a complete unknown at random from a directory.

94 HOLDING OPEN DAYS

If you are a new therapist or even an experienced therapist who has moved locations, you need to let as many people as possible know that you exist and what benefits you offer. A tried and tested method is to have an open day.

An open day is more applicable to a therapist who has rented or leased premises or a room in a complementary therapy practice. It probably would not be such a good idea for someone who practises from home.

The idea is to let everyone know that on a certain day between certain times your practice doors are open for the general public to come along and find out more about you and the therapy. This is the type of event where it is imperative to get the local newspapers, radio and even television stations involved. You will need the local media to run features on your practice and publicise the open day in advance. When the day arrives, you should encourage the local media to be there to see you interacting with potential customers and giving mini demonstrations.

The media will want to photograph you with people. If necessary, persuade friends, neighbours and relatives to be there so that when the photographers or TV crew arrive you have people on whom you can demonstrate. Even if no one turns up for your open day, other than the people you know, you will still have gained some free publicity. If you give some incentive and have this mentioned in the announcement about the open day, you will persuade more people to turn up.

Ideas for incentives

- A free 10-minute demonstration on a strictly 'first come first served' basis
- Free 10-minute visualisation tape to the first 25 people
- Get a 20% discount voucher if you book your first session on the day

Have someone assisting you and offering everyone coffee or tea as they arrive. Put a few plates of biscuits or snacks around to encourage a relaxed, informal atmosphere. Have some background music playing and a pleasant aroma to add to the ambience.

This is your chance to make the open day a time for dealing with people's objections and allow potential customers to meet you face to face. You get publicity which would ordinarily be very expensive and make yourself known to the local community quickly.

13

Miscellaneous

The places, occasions and opportunities that a therapist can use to market their business are only limited by their imagination.

95 WORKING AT CRAFT MARKETS

All around the country, mainly at the weekend, but sometimes during the week, craft fairs and markets are organised. The goods on sale range from odd pieces of pottery to the usual knitting and weaving produce. There are stalls that sell natural medicines including herbal, homeopathic and Chinese medicines along with the Bach flower remedies. The description of 'craft' can be taken to mean any art, skill or creation.

At some fairs there will be tarot card readers, crystals and other gemstones for sale and possibly a medium will offer advice. There is nothing to stop any alternative or complementary practitioner setting up a stall and offering their services.

It is best to view this arena as a place to promote your therapy skills and your practice as opposed to giving a full session. However, you should be able to create mini sessions or 'tasters' to recover your expenses for the day.

Examples of tasters

- Colour healer – give brief advice on the best colours for a person.

- Iridiologist – provide a brief analysis of someone's state of health.

- Crystal therapist – provide a check on the balance of the chakras.

- Acupressure therapist – manipulate some meridian points on the body in relation to a particular ailment.

All of these ideas are intended to give a flavour of the type of treatment you offer and arouse the curiosity of the general public. Make sure you make a nominal charge for these mini sessions. You will often find that demonstrating your therapy on one person will attract others to gather round and watch. As with other strategies, always have plenty of leaflets to distribute and be prepared to accept bookings for your therapy.

96 TAKING A STALL AT A HEALTH FAIR

Events such as fairs are becoming more and more popular with the general public. At health fairs and mind-body-spirit events there is an enormous range of therapies, products and other services. With the more organised and national health fairs there are also guest speakers and mini tutorials for attendees at extra cost.

The general set up at a health fair is for therapists, course producers, natural medicine shops and a few others to hire stalls for a day or series of days to display what they have to offer. Many stall holders recover the cost of the day by offering mini versions of their therapies. The product stalls will be selling oils, books, crystals and the like.

The better fairs can be quite expensive so it can be worthwhile splitting the costs of a stall with a colleague. Two aromatherapists could operate on a shift basis – one could provide short therapy tasters to passing trade, and the other sell essential oils or oil burners. Another strategy is to get together and share a stall with someone who is offering a completely different therapy from you.

You might consider providing a tutorial at the fair. This is a great way of getting your name and therapy known and

is likely to increase your chances of getting private clients.
Just be clear about why you are taking a stall at the fair. Is
it to earn some money while giving mini sessions? Is it to
encourage people to buy your latest self help book or to
see you privately? Of course it could be a combination of
all three, but if you are looking for private clients you will
need the fair to be in your locality whereas if you are
selling products or your book it doesn't matter where the
fair is located – within reason.

Initially attend the fair as a customer to research how it
is organised, the type of people who attend and the
competition. Do your homework first and it will increase
your chances of success.

(97) PUBLICISING YOUR PRACTICE IN LIBRARIES

When they want some information that is not available in
the home or through other means most people will turn to
that central and vast source of information, the library.
This establishment can be another way for people to find
out about you and can be an excellent addition to your
marketing strategy.

There are two methods to adopt with regard to having a
presence at your local library. One is the official way (with
permission) and the other is the unofficial way (assumed
permission).

With permission

The official way is to ask how you can add the details of
your practice to the library's system. This will usually result
in you being given a form to complete which will get you a
listing on a local services directory on the computer. Do
not expect to be inundated with clients from this source. It
is worthwhile spending the few minutes it takes to get
listed, but there are other more successful ways of using
your library.

Ask if you may put a poster up giving details of your
practice. Libraries have plenty of noticeboards. However,

just because there is plenty of space available, it doesn't necessarily mean that the head librarian will agree to your request. On most occasions they will refuse permission unless your poster includes something of interest to the local community. If you are giving free yoga classes to the over 65s or pregnant mothers you are more likely to succeed. If the poster only promotes your private practice you will normally be refused. Give consideration to how to get past this hurdle if you want an official presence.

A compromise would be to describe your voluntary work and its timetable but also to include details of your private practice. Something along the lines of:

FREE YOGA CLASS
For the unemployed only
at
Bloggs Community Rooms
1st Monday of each month
From 2pm to 3:30pm

Yoga can help **you** with
Stress, Memory and Concentration
For details telephone 597256

This does enough to satisfy the library's rules. The class you detail on the poster does not have to be something new. It can be something that you have been doing for some time. It is just a way of using what you are already doing to your best advantage.

Assumed permission
The unofficial approach is to assume you can put a poster up in the library. In other words, you do not ask permission. This does mean that it can become a 'cloak and dagger' operation – waiting for the right moment to place a

poster when no one is looking! The only risk you take by doing this is one of the staff spotting you and telling you that you need permission to do it, or the staff noticing the poster and taking it down.

Using brochure stands

Another method and probably one with a greater response rate is using your practice brochure. Libraries have a number of brochure and leaflet holders which are crammed with details of local events, groups, societies, health matters, support groups and much more. All you need to do is just place some of your brochures amongst these. The staff will not notice them but the users of the library will. This can be a very good source of new clients, particularly if you place leaflets in a number of different places within a library and at different libraries in the area.

In order to succeed in business, you do at times need to bend the rules a little. You are providing a worthwhile service and all you are doing is letting people know that you exist. That is what a library is for: providing information for the public about what is available to them.

98 ADVERTISING IN SPORTS CENTRES

A place where many people congregate or pass through each day is the local sports centre. People are at these centres to enjoy some physical activity and you can assume that they are interested in their health and in ways of staying healthy.

Capture their imagination and inform them what they will gain through your therapy and you will be rewarded with a crop of clients. Make it as easy as possible for them to find out about you. These centres always have carousels for holding leaflets about sports courses, classes and other events. They include leaflets detailing all the activities on offer at the centre. There will sometimes be other leaflet holders for leisure activities at places such as the local aerodrome, zoo and historical sites. Essentially, the facility to display your practice brochures is already provided. All you need to do is to fill it!

Some centres will not give you permission to display your brochures. Others will if you create a link between a sports activity and your therapy. The centre management will be more accepting of your leaflets if there is the connection between what you are offering and the centre's activities. One of the easiest associations is for the therapist who offers help for sports injuries and highlights this fact in their leaflet.

If you can't find a direct connection between sport and your therapy you can still gain customers from sports centres. As long as there isn't a notice saying otherwise, then just place your leaflets in the racks. Keep them neat and tidy and don't go overboard. The idea is to attract customers but not to get the leaflets removed. After some time of returning and restocking your leaflets as they get taken, you will find that the sports centre staff have also got used to seeing them there and will assume that permission has been granted for their display.

Focussing attracts clients

1. A Chinese herbalist can produce a leaflet stating how they can help with athletes foot.
2. A shiatsu practitioner can highlight how they can help with energy levels.
3. A psychotherapist can connect physical fitness with mental and emotional fitness.

If your sports centre is really friendly you may even persuade them to display your posters in the café, reception area and locker rooms and anywhere there is a noticeboard.

99 GIVING AWAY PROMOTIONAL FREEBIES

If there was a way of reminding someone of your existence every day, it would be a great marketing strategy. If your contact details were always handy, then the possibilities of increasing your client base would greatly improve. Here is a possible way of achieving all of this.

At any opportunity, give your clients some promotional item which has some benefit to them. The easiest item to give is a ballpoint pen. The pen is something the client can use but it also has a benefit for you. It includes your practice name and contact details. Every time that the pen is used your client is going to be reminded of you. If ever that client wants to pass on your details to someone else, all they have to do is reach for their pen. Although we lose pens all the time, in this particular case this loss can still work for you. We don't really lose pens as much as we leave them behind somewhere or lend them to other people and don't ask for them back. The good news is that a lost pen can generate more business for you. The new owner of the pen is going to see your details and may become a new client or pass them on to someone else.

Stationery companies have found ways of manufacturing these pens quite economically and so it won't cost you the earth to use this strategy. But a pen is just one type of promotional freebee. With a little creativity you could give away many other items that all increase your client-attracting potential.

Examples of promotional items

- Key fobs
- Mugs
- Balloons
- Mouse mats
- Calendars
- Diaries

PRODUCING BOOKMARKS

A give-away that is relatively cheap to produce and can provide a fresh batch of clients for your practice is a bookmark.

Have printed on reasonably thick paper or material, probably a minimum of 120gsm, a vertical oblong shape whose size is approximately 8 inches by 1½ inches. If you turn an A4 sheet to landscape format, you can get 7 bookmarks. They look exactly the same as those many of the major bookshops give away when a customer buys a book. The customer gets a bag with the bookshop's name on it and a bookmark. Every time the customer uses that bookmark when reading their new book they will be reminded of the shop they bought it from.

Likewise, your bookmark will drop a hint about your therapy and all the benefits you can provide. You can distribute these to all your local libraries. Each time someone borrows a book they get one of your bookmarks. You could also drop some off at your local bookshops. Not all bookshops provide this service and so the smaller ones will appreciate this benefit for their clients. You might even be able to negotiate to share the costs with a friendly bookstore with your details on one side and the store's details on the other.

Consider other places that have a supply of books. Provide some to your local colleges and universities which all have libraries of their own. When students take the books home from college your bookmark will go with them and provide more chances of gaining new clients. Also consider hospitals, hospices and other places, as well as corporate libraries.

 PUTTING FLYERS ON CAR WINDSCREENS

How many times when you have parked in a car park, has someone put a leaflet behind your wiper blade? The leaflet could advertise a party, a discount at another store, details of a local bazaar or any of multitude different events. Some people find these flyers annoying but they produce the same action from people: you have to pull the flyer out from under the wiper blade. Once you have it in your hand, curiosity dictates that you will take a quick look at its contents. Unless the design is good and appeals to the driver straightaway, the flyer ends up as rubbish very quickly.

If you decide to use this method of promotion you need to capture the imagination of the driver within five seconds. Use an emotionally charged headline. Depending on the type of problems you offer help with, here are examples that you could use:

Fed Up Being Stressed?

or

Learn How to Relax Anywhere, Anytime

or

Does Your Life Lack Purpose?

Your headline must be punchy and hit the target. The smaller detail on the flyer can go on to say what therapy you are offering and include any reasons to take action immediately. These can be time limited, such as '10% discount before 31st March' or 'Free relaxation tape with each session while stocks last!'. Don't forget a contact telephone number. You may not want to include your postal address.

With any large commercial concern, where the business involves serving people en masse, a car park will be provided.

Examples of places with car parks

- Council run car parks

- Supermarkets

- Fast food chains

- Golf clubs

- Hardware stores

- Cinemas and Theatres

- Pubs and wine bars

Most flyer deliverers do not ask permission. They just get on with it. If a supermarket or other business telephones and asks you not to do this in their car park, then you can comply with their request. Until such time, you can carry on attracting clients.

You do not have to make special trips to all the car parks in the area, although this can be done if you want to blitz a place. Why not have some handy in your car? The next time you use a car park, just go around and distribute your flyers.

 ATTRACTING PASSING TRADE

In this modern hi tech age of computers, the Internet and television we sometimes forget that some of the old trusted methods can still reap rewards.

Plaques help marketing

Lawyers, doctors, dentists, accountants and other professionals like to have some form of plaque at their place of business. In the past this has been brass and has been inscribed with the person's name, designations and profession and maybe a telephone number. These plaques are usually positioned near the front door of the business premises.

The purpose of the plaque can be twofold. Firstly, for people who have booked an appointment it confirms that they have arrived at the correct address. It can also add to the professionalism that the client expects. Secondly it may attract passing trade. Some businesses place their plaque at the first entrance to the property grounds such as the gate. Again, it serves to confirm that new clients have arrived at the correct address but also it advertises the type of business that operates at these premises. This could produce the effect that people passing the plaque may either call in to find out more, or make a note of the telephone number and call for details.

Therapists who operate from their own private residence may not want passing trade calling in without an appointment or neighbours to know their business. If your home looks too much as if a business is being run from it, then the local authorities may want to charge you a business rate. For some a plaque may not be a good idea, but for the rest it is an acceptable form of promotion and, once purchased, will not drain any more funds from your marketing budget.

Other options

There are other ways of attracting people passing by your practice premises. Many shop retailers use a free standing noticeboard to attract customers. They put this outside during business hours and bring it back in when closing for the day. This gives a better chance of informing people that you exist and your location. It can be particularly essential if you operate from premises that do not have a shop front but only a single anonymous door leading to your practice. You may need to get permission from the local authorities before using a noticeboard as it will be standing on a pedestrian path.

ADVERTISING ON CARS

Next time you are in a car park have a look at the stickers that people put on their cars. In the UK these will mainly be placed on the windows. They give free advertising to car insurers or holiday destinations and so on – or can be some humorous prose. How many times have you seen a beat up old jalopy with the sticker saying 'My other car is a Rolls Royce'? These stickers do get noticed.

Marketing via other people's cars

Consider designing a tasteful sticker of your own. These can be placed on your car, your partner's, or friends' and relatives' cars. Every time you see a new client give them a sticker for their car. Every time you send a mail pack include a sticker. Stickers are cheap to produce and you will need to give quite a few away to see some reward.

The design of the sticker is very important. It needs to catch someone's eye quickly and get them to take action. Like any form of copy, it needs to have an emotional impact.

If you have a memorable telephone number, this can really make a difference with car stickers. Something like 0800 RELAX would be fantastic for many therapists but even something like 0800 93 83 73 can be just as successful. Most therapists will have their standard telephone number. In this case you will have to rely on someone having a good memory or of them going to the trouble of writing it down.

Signs on your car

In the US, you can obtain car plates that promote your business. Football fanatics may show which team they follow with a plate showing COWBOYS, for the Dallas Cowboys. Students may have a plate showing the university they attend. Why not promote your practice with a sign alongside your registration plate?

If you really feel bold, you can always invest in a magnetic sign that sticks to the side of the two front doors of your car or people carrier. Whenever you go on a trip for shopping or to the cinema for example, you can put your magnetic sign up and your car becomes a mobile promotional vehicle. When you get back home, you simply take the signs off and your car becomes a normal private vehicle.

(104) GIVE THEM MORE!

Your client's trust in you and your therapy is priceless. Getting your client's trust means that you are only a short step away from gaining their belief in your skills. Belief counts for a lot in any aspect of life but is particularly useful in the healing profession. Incredible as it might seem, some clients arrive with no belief in your therapy. They are there because conventional medicine has failed them and you are a last resort. They have hope more than belief at this stage.

If we feel valued as individuals or collectively, it boosts our esteem. It helps us to believe that we matter. Help your client feel that they are the most important person in the world to you during the therapy session. If you make them your centre of attention they will feel valued.

Any client will have in a mind a rough idea of what they expect to get for their money. Give them any less and they will begrudge the money they have spent. Give them more and they will feel happy and attach a greater value to your service.

Adding extra value to your service

* If a client has booked for an hour and you haven't quite completed the therapy, give them a little extra time (if your schedule permits). Some therapists tell clients that a session lasts an hour but always give a 70-minute session. The client gets an extra 10 minutes and will come to the conclusion that you are more interested in helping them than your fee.

- Provide your client with a complimentary cassette tape of relaxation music.

- Provide a printout of 'tips and advice' that may also assist the resolution of a problem (e.g a colonic irrigation practitioner might provide dietary tips to aid recovery from IBS).

- Give copies of Internet articles to educate the client more about their condition.

- Offer telephone and/or email support at an agreed time. You might even be more proactive and telephone them to get a progress report.

The above examples illustrate how you can surpass your client's expectations of your service. Giving them something more than they expect adds value to your service in their eyes. The added value that they feel can lead to them having more of that powerful resource, belief.

Oh yes. I don't know if you have noticed, but this book is subtitled '101 tried and tested ways to attract clients'. This is number 104! Do make sure your client notices the added extras, otherwise they will be wasted.

14

A Winning Strategy

In order to keep a steady stream of enquiries, you should market your practice every week. That means *every* week. If you stop marketing when you are experiencing a feast of clients then you will soon experience a famine. Some marketing methods require a longer lead time to get a response, maybe weeks or months. Others can be rewarding very quickly – literally within hours. If you continue to market your practice every week you give yourself what every therapist craves, a reliable flow of new clients week after week and financial security.

Follow this A.C.T.I.O.N. formula:

Activity
What is the activity or action you need to do to promote your business?

Communicate
It is most important to get all aspects of your communication right. What message are you trying to communicate on the telephone, in a letter, when greeting clients to your practice, in your promotions?

Tenacity
Keep going. Persistence pays. While others may fall by the wayside, you will succeed by pursuing your marketing goals.

Inventive
Dare to be different. Don't only imitate what is good but improve on it. Use your creative skills in every task you tackle.

Opportunity

Be an opportunity taker. Look for the opportunities in everything you come across. You can make your own luck.

Now

Tomorrow never comes. Don't leave things so long that your ideas are actioned by someone else and you find yourself saying 'I was thinking of doing that'. While you are thinking about it others may be doing it. Take action today!

If you get more enquiries than you can handle, you can always start a waiting list. Although your intention is to help people as soon as possible it is sometimes impractical to see everyone. If you have to start a waiting list it also adds to the perception of a therapist who is so successful that people are willing to wait to see them. Of course you can always refer your excess clients to colleagues. Your colleagues will think you are fantastic because you are giving them business and the client gets to see a therapist sooner.

Set your sights on attracting a certain number of clients each week and make the target achievable. As you reach a target set a new target until you attract the number of clients you are comfortable with each week. Never worry about over marketing yourself.

Monitoring your marketing

Next to your accounting and client case histories, one of your most important administration tasks is to record how successful your marketing has been. Whenever you see a new client always ask them how they heard about you. This should be one of the questions on your case history form anyway. But don't leave that particular piece of information there. At the end of the week transfer the details of how your client found you to your marketing monitoring records. This literally takes five minutes but can save you an amazing amount of time, wasted energy and money.

Invest in a book of blank pages and head each page with details of the marketing method, the date started and how much, if anything, it cost you. For example:

Yellow Pages April 2000 to March 2001 Cost £1,200   **Page 1**

Date	Client Name	Session Fee	Number of Sessions	Total
03 Jan 02	Fred Smith	£70	llll	£280
04 Jan 02	Mary Bloggs	£70	ll	£140

Library Leaflet   April 2001   Cost FREE   Page 2

Date	Client Name	Session Fee	Number of Sessions	Total
07 Feb 02	Joy Grange	£120	1	£120

From the above records you will soon see how well each marketing method is working for you. Keeping a total of the fees enables you to calculate quickly when you will be in profit with each method.

Keeping records of personal recommendations is also important because it acts as a notice from the client that they still remain very happy with the therapy they received from you. You may also want to drop them a note to thank them for their referrals. Your appreciation will encourage them to continue sending you more clients.

Analyse, adjust and repeat

Give each marketing method a set period for attracting clients. Once the period has ended, subtract the costs from the total of the clients' fees. You will then be left with either a profit, loss or break even figure.

If you have a profit then repeat this particular marketing strategy. If this strategy was a newspaper advertisement, for example, unless some aspect has been an obvious error do not be tempted to change it significantly. Even though you may be bored with it because you have seen it so many times, the public will not have. In fact, even though this may be your second, third or fourth run of this advert, many people will be seeing it for the first time.

Strategies that break even may still be counted as one of your successes. Remember that the new clients came to you through this may well recommend you to others in the future. So over a longer period of time you may find that this method moves from break even to profit. With break even strategies you should consider some minor changes but also consider running the promotion again as it is. Even some of the most successful strategies will, on occasions, bring in less than expected responses. This can be due to external factors like the season, Christmas, Easter, summer holiday time or other reasons.

With those strategies that disappoint – or in other words do not pay for themselves – you should make wholesale changes before trying them out again. There is a good possibility that with significant changes you can make this strategy a winning one. Some of the most successful marketing methods start out as the poorest but it is important to get as much value as possible from any strategy you use. The value from a strategy that fails is the lessons you learn.

It could be that a trade show costs you money and brings in very few customers. Rather than deciding that trade shows do not work, you must analyse how you ran your stall. Ask yourself questions like, 'What did I do that I could have done better?', 'What were my fellow stall holders doing?', 'Which stall holders seemed to be doing well and why?'. By answering these questions you may find solutions that will give you the confidence to attend another trade show – but this time be much better prepared.

When you have analysed every aspect of a particular marketing method that has not achieved the desired effect and you feel that no matter what you do, it never will, then drop it. Your winning marketing strategy must be to repeat what works for you, analyse and adjust what disappoints and drop what doesn't work.

Remember, it doesn't matter how fanatastic a therapist you are, if potential clients don't know that you exist, your practice cannot be successful. Marketing is absolutely crucial to your business. Try out the ideas in this book, find which ones work best for you and add to them using your imagination. Good luck!

Index

Contents